Eliza

Miss E. R. Snow

Eliza

THE LIFE AND FAITH
OF ELIZA R. SNOW

KAREN LYNN DAVIDSON AND JILL MULVAY DERR

DESERET
BOOK

SALT LAKE CITY, UTAH

Library of Congress Cataloging-in-Publication Data
Davidson, Karen Lynn, author.
  Eliza: The Life and Faith of Eliza R. Snow / Karen Lynn Davidson and Jill Mulvay Derr.
      pages cm
  Includes bibliographical references and index.
  ISBN 978-1-60908-902-3 (hardbound : alk. paper) 1. Snow, Eliza R. (Eliza Roxcy), 1804–1887. 2. Mormon women—Biography. 3. Mormons—United States—Biography. 4. Poets, American—19th century—Biography. I. Derr, Jill Mulvay, author. II. Title.
  BX8695.S745D38 2013
  289.3092—dc23
  [B]   2012017495

Printed in China
R. R. Donnelley, Shenzhen, China

10 9 8 7 6 5 4 3 2 1

Contents

PREFACE

What can Latter-day Saints draw from the life and writings of Eliza R. Snow? Certainly she is an icon of faith, one of the best known of all Mormon pioneer women. We hear her name often as an example of strength and devotion, and we sing her beloved hymns. When we ponder the precious Latter-day Saint teaching concerning a Mother in Heaven, we think immediately of "O My Father." In photographs, with her serene expression and her far-seeing eyes that gaze at us across so many decades, Eliza Snow truly looks like the legend she has become.

Sometimes a legend can seem so distant in time, in circumstances so unlike our own, and the life so impossibly heroic, that we might wonder whether the woman behind the legend can really offer us anything to inspire and enrich our own lives. In fact, although the joys and sorrows of women's lives today may differ from those Eliza experienced, the responses and solutions remain largely the same. She spoke out boldly about her beliefs, and she reached out to others. When hardship came her way, she made the best of her circumstances; at a particularly difficult moment on the trail to Winter Quarters—a "growling, grumbling, devilish, sickly time"—she resolved "to see the game thro,' & enjoy the scenery."

Many women and men, in reading her poems, have felt that Eliza really knew what it is like to lose a loved one, or to rejoice in friendship, or to suffer under injustice, or to love one's country, or to overflow with testimony and gratitude. Such experiences are universal among Latter-day Saints, and Eliza's writings let us know, poem by poem and journal entry by journal entry, that she would understand us nearly perfectly. For our part, we can understand her as well, especially as we come to know her better through her life story and her writings.

Like all those who have become legends, Eliza R. Snow was courageous, resourceful, dedicated, and persuasive. And to this list we add the additional traits that so endear her to us as a woman of God: her unflagging testimony of the Prophet Joseph Smith and of his prophetic successors, her willingness to sacrifice for the kingdom, her commitment to developing women's spiritual strength, her love for temples and temple work, and her ever-present vision of the destiny of the Saints as the Lord's chosen people of the latter days. These values shine through Eliza's poetry.

Many do not realize that the poetry of Eliza R. Snow is far more than the hymn texts we love. Among her more than five hundred poems are funeral tributes, reflections on home and family, rhymed sermons, nature poems, tributes to her many close friends, playful songs, and complicated epics. Sometimes a private emotion or impulse sparked the idea for a poem. At other times, she was called upon to be a spokeswoman on behalf of the Saints, and thus her words helped the early members of the Church, in times of success and in times of trial, to form their image of themselves and their mission.

Born on January 21, 1804, in Becket, Massachusetts, Eliza was the second daughter of fifth-generation New Englanders Oliver and Rosetta Pettibone Snow. When Eliza was almost two years old, the family moved to Mantua, Ohio, where Eliza was to live for almost three decades. The Snows were financially successful, civic-minded, and well respected. Oliver and Rosetta Snow taught all their children—five more were to be born into the family—to be responsible and hard-working, and they encouraged their daughters as well as their sons to read and become educated. Eliza worked as a secretary in the office of her father, who was a successful farmer and justice of the peace, and she was employed as a seamstress and schoolteacher as well.

Even as a schoolgirl, Eliza loved to read and write poetry. In 1825, when she was twenty-one, her first published poem appeared in the Ravenna, Ohio, *Western Courier*. Thus began a poetic career that was to continue for more than sixty years.

In the early months of 1831, the Snow family's friend and minister, Sidney Rigdon, introduced them to Joseph Smith. Soon thereafter Eliza's sister Leonora and their mother, Rosetta, joined the Church, but Eliza and other family members held back. More than four years later, after much thought and study, the thirty-one-year-old Eliza entered the waters of baptism, and from that moment on she placed her poetic gifts at the service of the Church. She soon moved to nearby Kirtland, Ohio, to join with the Saints.

Once she had cast her lot with Joseph Smith and his followers, Eliza experienced the dangers and privations that marked so much of early Latter-day Saint history. Accustomed to comfort and security, she now faced uncertainty. In the spring of 1838, as neighboring Ohioans began to object to the Saints' increasing political influence and as economic collapse faced Kirtland, she left Kirtland to settle with her family and her fellow Saints in northern Missouri. In 1839, the rising threats and persecution in Missouri left the Saints no choice but to flee the state, and the Snows joined the exodus to Illinois. There, on the banks of the Mississippi, the Saints founded the city of Nauvoo.

Under the direction of Joseph Smith, the industry of the Saints produced a large, well-ordered city with a beautiful temple under construction. There Eliza's life changed significantly when, in June 1842, she was sealed—married by priesthood authority—as a plural wife to the Prophet Joseph Smith. Within a few years, Joseph Smith's nontraditional teachings and the Saints' melding of civic and religious authority antagonized neighbors and even some Church members. Once again, intense conflict threatened the safety and liberty of the Saints. Joseph Smith was murdered on June 27, 1844, and Eliza mourned the loss of the man she had loved as both prophet and husband. Eventually the Saints were forced to abandon their city, their homes, and their temple. They began their trek westward under the leadership of Brigham Young, to whom Eliza had been married as a plural wife in October 1844. After a short stay in Winter Quarters, she arrived in the Salt Lake Valley on October 2, 1847.

In Salt Lake City, the name of Eliza R. Snow became increasingly well known as her poetry appeared in hymnals and in the Saints' *Deseret News*. She wrote hymns of praise, encouragement, and admonition; she wrote farewell tributes to missionaries and then welcomed them home again; she celebrated personal occasions, such as friends' birthdays, and public occasions, such as the Fourth of July; she placed national and world events within the context of the restored gospel.

In addition to writing poetry, Eliza gradually assumed other public responsibilities. In Nauvoo, she had kept minutes of the first meetings of the Female Relief Society of

Nauvoo. Later, in Utah Territory, as a trusted assistant to Brigham Young, she played a central role in the revival of Relief Society. She eventually became its second general president and traveled and spoke widely throughout the territory. Working with other women, she helped to organize associations for young women and children and to establish a Latter-day Saint women's newspaper and hospital. Admired as a leader and administrator, she was likewise well known for her service in the Endowment House, where temple ordinances for the living were performed before the Salt Lake Temple was completed. The many hours she spent there each week were one of the joys of her life.

Eliza was also a caring family member and friend. As a plural wife of Joseph Smith and then of Brigham Young and also as the sister of Lorenzo Snow, she enjoyed ties to three large and prominent families, enhancing her influence and enlarging the circle of her connections. From her move as a new convert to Kirtland, Ohio, in 1836 until her death as "Zion's Poetess" and "Presidentess" in Salt Lake City, Utah Territory, on December 5, 1887, Eliza R. Snow cherished personal relationships and celebrated her connection to the community of Latter-day Saints.

This book introduces readers to Eliza R. Snow through a survey of her life, a sampling of her poetry, and an array of visual images. These elements vividly render the joys, hopes, and sorrows of Eliza and her fellow Saints, conveying us into an earlier and very different world. At the same time, in this mix of fortitude and testimony, humor, reflection, and association, today's Saints will recognize much that is familiar.

The narrative draws upon a rich variety of sources, including Eliza R. Snow's published and unpublished poems, her diaries (1842–1844 and 1846–1849), her "Sketch of My Life" (1885), and her prose articles and discourses. The poems featured here, as well as some of the narrative text, have been drawn from *Eliza R. Snow: The Complete Poetry*, edited by Jill Mulvay Derr and Karen Lynn Davidson (Provo and Salt Lake City: Brigham Young University Press and University of Utah Press, 2009). That volume contains annotations and introductions to the poems, including dates of composition, alternate titles, and dates of publication, as well as an extensive list of works cited that reflects a substantial body of scholarship on Eliza R. Snow spanning nearly forty years. The authors are particularly indebted to BYU Press for support in the completion of that work, which has served as the parent volume of *Eliza: The Life and Faith of Eliza R. Snow.*

ACKNOWLEDGMENTS

The contributions of many generous people over the years have made this book possible. Although they are too numerous to thank individually, special appreciation is due to several whose support and encouragement have been essential. Suzanne Brady, managing editor at Deseret Book, is a true kindred spirit whose enthusiasm, experience, and insights have been invaluable. Shauna Gibby, designer, and Rachael Ward, typographer, have created a lovely book; Eliza R. Snow, with her keen eye for beauty, would surely be pleased.

We are indebted to Maureen Ursenbach Beecher, whose work on Eliza R. Snow, in particular *The Personal Writings of Eliza R. Snow*, enhanced our knowledge and made conveniently available some of Eliza's most important writings. We also thank the capable people at Brigham Young University Press, in particular John W. Welch, editor-in-chief of *BYU Studies*, and Heather Seferovich, senior executive editor, for their untiring work in bringing to completion *Eliza R. Snow: The Complete Poetry*. For her help with that volume and for her assistance in earlier stages of the present book, we express our warm gratitude to Jennifer Reeder. In addition, we note with appreciation that the Church History Department of The Church of Jesus Christ of Latter-day Saints has provided significant support over many years for scholarship focused on Eliza R. Snow and related historical topics.

Most of all, we acknowledge with gratitude the encouragement and patience of our husbands, David A. Davidson and C. Brooklyn Derr. Their steady support unfailingly reflects the "order and concord, harmony and love" Eliza Snow describes in her poem "Eden" (*Complete Poetry*, 97–98).

CHRONOLOGY

JANUARY 21, 1804	Born in Becket, Berkshire Co., Massachusetts
1805	Snow family moves to Mantua, Portage Co., Ohio
AUGUST 13, 1825	Publication of first poem, "Pity &c.," *Western Courier,* Ravenna, Portage Co., Ohio
c. 1828	Baptized a member of the primitivist Christian congregation at Mantua, Ohio (later Disciples of Christ)
WINTER 1830–31	Met Joseph Smith at her parents' home, Mantua, Ohio
APRIL 5, 1835	Baptized a member of the Church of the Latter Day Saints
DECEMBER 1835	Moved to Kirtland, Geauga Co., Ohio
SPRING 1838	Moved to Adam-ondi-Ahman, Caldwell Co., Missouri
MARCH 1839	Moved to Illinois
MARCH 17, 1842	Organization of the Female Relief Society of Nauvoo; ERS elected secretary
JUNE 29, 1842	Married and sealed to Joseph Smith
JUNE 27, 1844	Martyrdom of Joseph and Hyrum Smith
OCTOBER 3, 1844	Married Brigham Young
OCTOBER 1845	Wrote "O My Father"
OCTOBER 2, 1847	Arrived in the Salt Lake Valley

CHRONOLOGY

MAY 1855	Called by Brigham Young to preside over women's ordinance work in the Salt Lake Endowment House
1856	*Poems, Religious, Historical, and Political* (vol. 1) published in Liverpool, England
1856	Moved into Lion House, where Brigham Young's family lived
APRIL 1868	Called to assist in reestablishing ward Relief Societies, Utah Territory
MAY 1870	Assisted in organizing Young Ladies Retrenchment Society, Salt Lake City
OCTOBER 26, 1872– JULY 1873	Traveled to Europe and Palestine with Lorenzo Snow, George A. Smith, and others; *Correspondence of Palestine Tourists* published 1875
AUGUST 29, 1877	Death of Brigham Young
1877	*Poems, Religious, Historical, and Political* (vol. 2) published in Salt Lake City
AUGUST 1878	Assisted in organizing the Primary Association, Farmington (17 miles north of Salt Lake City)
JUNE–JULY 1880	Called and set apart as general president of the Relief Society, Salt Lake City
1880	*Children's Primary Hymn Book* and *Children's Primary Tune Book* (edited by ERS) published in Salt Lake City
1881	*Bible Questions and Answers* published in Salt Lake City
1882	*Primary Speaker Book One* and *Primary Speaker Book Two* (edited by ERS) published in Salt Lake City
1884	*Biography and Family Record of Lorenzo Snow* published in Salt Lake City
AUGUST 24 , 1887	Wrote "Evening Thoughts" (last poem)
DECEMBER 5, 1887	Died in Salt Lake City
DECEMBER 7, 1887	Funeral held in Assembly Hall, Salt Lake City

Eliza R. Snow.

Chapter One

My Heart Is Fixed

1804–1835

Eliza Roxcy Snow was not only a talented child but a fortunate one. The love and encouragement of her family surrounded her from the time she was born, and she knew she had been blessed. In an unpublished poem recorded in her journal, she expressed her tender feelings about home:

> Home, charming sound—the name is sweet:
>> O what, on earth is half so dear?
> At home the social feelings meet—
>> The kind affections center here.[1]

As we look back in time, it seems that the Lord in his wisdom often provided the home, the family, and the opportunities that prepared individuals to assume their future roles in the restoration and growth of the Church. The parents and siblings of the Prophet Joseph Smith were students of the Bible, religious seekers who helped and encouraged the young Joseph as the truths of the Restoration were revealed to him. Even their financial struggles could well have played a role in forming the compassionate

---

1. Lines 1–4 of "Home, Charming Sound," a poem of 24 lines. Snow copied the poem into her journal, but it was not published. See *Complete Poetry*, 51–52.

Opposite: *Eliza's signature beneath her portrait.*

adult who became the Prophet. Brigham Young learned skilled carpentry as a youth and was in business for himself at the age of twenty-one; he built upon this early experience to later direct the colonization of scores of settlements in the Mountain West. George Careless, to whom we owe the tunes of such well-loved hymns as "The Morning Breaks" and "Prayer Is the Soul's Sincere Desire," was trained at the Royal Academy of London.[2] He emigrated to Salt Lake City in 1864, well prepared to make his mark on the musical history of the Church.

What about Eliza R. Snow? What were the early family influences that helped form this remarkable poet and leader? Neither she nor her family could have imagined her future place in history, the unique and public roles that would one day be hers. In future years, any important visitor to Salt Lake City was likely to be introduced to "Zion's Poetess," the famous Eliza R. Snow. At the direction of Brigham Young, she helped to organize the Relief Society among the Saints in the West and served as its general president. Indeed, she essentially presided also over the work of the Young Ladies' Retrenchment or Mutual Improvement Association and the Primary Association, both of which she had helped to organize. "She did more for the Womanhood of the Church [than] any woman before or since her time," wrote Susa Young Gates.[3] Even such a precocious child as Eliza could not have envisioned such a destiny.

Yet the influences and encouragement that surrounded Eliza as she grew to womanhood proved in many ways to be an ideal preparation for her future life. Eliza Snow grew up in the new American republic. Her Snow and Pettibone grandfathers had fought in the Revolutionary War, and the young nation was pushing westward to new land. In 1805, Eliza's parents, Oliver and Rosetta Pettibone Snow, took their two young daughters from Becket, Massachusetts, to the Western Reserve in northeastern Ohio. Thomas Jefferson was president of the United States when the Snows cleared heavily timbered land at Mantua, near Kirtland, to construct a log cabin. In 1815,

---

2. *Hymns* (1985), nos. 1 and 145.

3. "Life in the Lion House," Susa Young Gates Collection, Box 12, fd. 2, p. 40, Utah State Historical Society, Salt Lake City.

The Oliver and Rosetta Pettibone Snow home in Mantua, Ohio.

Oliver and Rosetta moved their growing family into a frame house in Mantua, the home where Eliza resided for almost thirty years. She was the second of her parents' seven children; four daughters were followed by three sons. Her siblings, born between 1801 and 1821, were Leonora Abigail, Percy Amanda, Melissa, Lorenzo, Lucius Augustus, and Samuel Pearce (or Pierce).

In her brief autobiography, written in 1877 and revised in 1885 as "Sketch of My Life," Eliza tells us that her mother "considered a practical knowledge of housekeeping the best, and most efficient foundation on which to build a magnificent structure of womanly accomplishments—that useful knowledge was the most reliable basis of independence."[4] Thus Eliza and her sisters were "early trained to the kitchen and housekeeping in general; then to various kinds of needlework <u>etc.</u>"[5]

---

4. Snow, "Sketch," in Beecher, *Personal Writings,* 6.
5. Snow, "Sketch," in Beecher, *Personal Writings,* 6.

But the education of the Snow daughters went beyond these traditional female accomplishments. At a time when many families lacked the means or desire to educate their daughters, "our parents extended to us the best educational facilities attainable at that time," she records, "without preference to either sex."[6] Her "inherent fondness for reading," she adds, "was encouraged by my parents. I was partial to poetical works."[7] Her home was a place of "book-studies and schooling . . . music and singing."[8] Formal classroom education was enriched with reading and study at home, as was typical for many families of this period.

Such a background served her well in later years. A confident and self-assured Eliza, knowing that her reading and education would enable her to converse with almost anyone she met, could comfortably entertain visitors to Salt Lake City, travel abroad, speak to large gatherings, and express herself fluently in both poetry and prose.

Furthermore, in a stroke of good fortune that would rarely have been available for a girl in the early 1800s, Eliza had the opportunity to work in a professional setting. Her father held several positions over the years as justice of the peace and county commissioner, and although such a post at that time would usually have been given to a young man, he employed Eliza as his assistant, or "Secretary." In this way she was introduced to the world of contracts, finances, and official documents. As she notes in "Sketch of My Life," "This experience has proved of great benefit to myself and to others, at different periods of my variegated life."[9] This "great benefit" of her office work can well be imagined. When she shouldered heavy organizational responsibilities in temple service, Relief Society, the children's Primary Association, the Woman's

---

6. Snow, "Sketch," in Beecher, *Personal Writings,* 6.
7. Snow, "Sketch," in Beecher, *Personal Writings,* 7.
8. Snow, "Sketch," in Beecher, *Personal Writings,* 7.
9. Snow, "Sketch," in Beecher, *Personal Writings,* 6.

OPPOSITE: *This is the earliest known photograph of Eliza, a daguerreotype photograph taken in the 1850s. In the background are the manuscripts of three unpublished poems, taken from her journal: "My Home & My Harp" (1830), "The Parting" (undated), and "To W. A. S. [William Alexander Smith]" (1853)* (Complete Poetry, *30–31, 70–71, 442–443).*

My Home & my Harp.

At the soft evening twilight
I dearly love to gaze
Upon the landscape scenery
As Spring moves on apace.

O, what is so delightful
As this beloved spot,
Where the great Arbiter of fate
Has cast my happy lot.

Here, pass'd my sunny childhood
And here, I fain would spend
My days of youth and womanhood,
Or life, till life shall end.

When ...
Beneath a distant ...

This flowing, sunny landscape
In nature's grandeur spread,
Will meet no more my raptur'd gaze,
Nor my delighted tread.

But nature's gifts are ample,
And landscapes far away
Perchance will seem as beautiful—
Perchance will look as gay.

And when I gaze upon them
In all their summer pride;
They'll seem to speak of days gone by
When thou wert by my side.

W. N. S.

ating.

And when the twilight breeze,
Move placidly along;
I'll think of the rich melodies
That grac'd our evening song.

And when night's circling shadows
Shall hide earth's canopy;
With fervor shall my heart and voice
Ascend to God for thee.

The carriage now is ready
And waiting at the door—
Farewel, farewel! we're parting n
Perhaps to meet no more!

Mantua, Portage-co, Ohio,

Expressions of friendship, as proffer'd by you,
Are like pearls, found on life's rugged road;
Like a bright summer-blossom, bespangled with dew,
Is a favor, in kindness bestow'd.

That prosperity, health, and long life may be given
You, and peace & salvation attend;
While securing, in time, the rich treasure of heaven
Is the wish of your sister and friends

And the life-likeness pow'r of daguerrean art
More forcibly, nought has defin'd;
Than the impress of gratitude, form'd in the heart
From a noble, ingenuous mind.

Commission Store, and on the board of the Deseret Hospital Association, she was well able to carry out such duties. Though her early experience had been on a much smaller scale, she knew she could comfortably work with both men and women and in many different spheres.

As a child, Eliza refined her poetic skills in private. She sometimes wrote her school lessons in rhyme, and she "frequently made attempts at imitations of the different styles of favorite authors."[10] None of these earliest poems have survived in either manuscript or printed form, but in August 1825, when she was twenty-one years old, her first published poem appeared in the Ravenna, Ohio, *Western Courier*. The *Western Courier* and the *Ohio Star,* both weekly papers published at Ravenna, Ohio, the seat of Portage County, carried thirty-three of Eliza's poems between 1825 and 1832. Another nine poems from this period, unpublished, have come down to us in her handwriting.

These early poems, written when Eliza was in her twenties or early thirties, are not the poems of a beginner. Her range of subject and meter is amazing. Certainly her earliest work points toward a future as a prolific and versatile poet. In addition, these poems are almost the only record we have of her thoughts and experiences from her childhood to her young womanhood. No journal or letters exist for this period, and her autobiographical reminiscence deals only briefly with these earliest years.

Some excerpts from a few of Eliza's early poems will show how different they could be from one another and how she chose distinctive and appropriate verse forms for different topics. The poetic form known as blank verse became her choice for some of her finest poems.[11] "Eloquence," a poem in blank verse published in 1829, begins with one of her most lyrical responses to the beauties of nature:

> *There is an eloquence that breathes thro' out*
> *The world inanimate. There is a tone,*

---

10. Snow, "Sketch," in Beecher, *Personal Writings,* 7.
11. See page 39 herein.

A silent tone of speech that meets the soul
And whispers things pathetic, soft and sweet:
Like the enchantments of the night which move
On slumber's downy chariot wheels, and dress
In playfulness of mirth the hours of rest.[12]

Some of Eliza's early poems addressed subjects that were typical for the female poets of the day, such as friendship, home, and family. One was titled "Friendship," another "Home, Charming Sound" (stanza 1 is quoted at the beginning of this chapter), another "To My Box-Wood Blossoms."[13] Other early poems, however, were lofty, high-minded verse patterned on such models as the British poets John Milton and Alexander Pope, with the most serious national or world events as their subjects. When Eliza learned of the Turkish conquest of Missolonghi, a city on the west coast of Greece that withstood the enemy bravely during the Greek fight for independence, she was moved to write an impassioned expression of sorrow, highlighting in part the heartbreak of the Grecian women:

Weep now; nor blush to weep, while ye lament
How bled the matron and the maid of Greece.

   See with what anxious tenderness she plies,
Unmindful of the grief that swells her heart,
Some healing balm—some kind restorative
To save a husband, brother, or a sire,
On whose joint efforts hang the fate of Greece.[14]

---

12. Lines 1–7 of "Eloquence," a 68-line poem published in *Western Courier,* June 19, 1829. Snow later revised and expanded the poem, including it in *Poems* (1877). See *Complete Poetry,* 28–30.

13. "Friendship," "Home, Charming Sound," and "To My Box-Wood Blossoms," in *Complete Poetry,* 35–36, 51–52, and 38, respectively.

14. Lines 10–11 and 15–19 of "Missolonghi," a 37-line poem dated July 13, 1826, and published in *Western Courier,* July 22, 1826. See *Complete Poetry,* 9–11.

Often Eliza used a more familiar rhymed meter, even for a serious subject. An 1830 poem shows her strong feelings concerning justice and human rights. On December 8, 1829, in his first message to Congress, President Andrew Jackson strongly advocated the forced removal of the American Indians to a designated area west of the Mississippi. Both the House of Representatives and the Senate soon introduced Indian removal bills. Eliza was outraged. She wrote "The Red Man of the West," voicing the plight of the Indians:

> *The Great Spirit, 'tis said, to our forefathers gave*
> *All the lands 'twixt the eastern and western big wave,*
> *And the Indian was happy, he'd nothing to fear,*
> *As he rang'd o'er the mountains in chase of the deer:*
> *Say then was he homeless? No, no his heart beat*
> *For the dear ones he lov'd in the wigwam retreat.*
> *But a wreck of the white man came over the wave,*
> *In the chains of the tyrant he'd learn'd to enslave:*
> *Emerging from bondage, and pale with distress,*
> *He fled from oppression, he came to oppress!*
> *Chas'd into environs, and no where to fly,*
> *Too weak to contend, and unwilling to die,*
> *Oh where will a place for the Indian be found?*
> *Shall he take to the skies? or retreat under ground?*[15]

Experimenting always with different meters, voices, and topics, Eliza gradually built her personal and literary identity. As a young woman in her twenties, she addressed themes of faith, patriotism, responsibility, and alienation, and explored

15. Lines 1–4, 9–14, and 31–34 of "The Red Man of the West," a 34-line poem published in *Ohio Star*, March 31, 1830. Snow later revised and expanded the poem and gave it a new title, "The Lamanite." See *Complete Poetry*, 33–34.

questions regarding oppression, gender roles, and life beyond death. All these topics would recur repeatedly in her work throughout her life.

Eliza loved nature and the land—the "flowing, sunny landscape" of the Ohio frontier. Her father, in addition to his public duties, was a successful farmer, and her mother a farmer's wife. In 1828, Eliza composed a delightful poem called "The Farmer's Wife." Although it may seem to be an overly simple, sentimental notion of rural joys, this poem is deeper than it first appears. The praise of the farmer's wife echoes Proverbs 31, the tribute to the virtuous woman whose "price is far above rubies."[16]

The Farmer's Wife

If there's a smile on nature's face
It is the farmer's dwelling place—
If house-wife has whereof to boast
The farmer's wife may claim the most.
The richest products of the soil,
The finest wheat, the wine and oil—
The fruits, the dainties of the land,
Are at the farmer's wife's command.

The wool and flax which he provides,
She manufactures and divides
Among her household as they need.
She's blest in blessing—rich indeed!
Well busied at the wheel and loom
Her constant feet abide at home:
Her husband's heart rewards her toil,
Without distrust—no fear of spoil.

Well skill'd in all domestic cares—
Content to mind her own affairs—
What truly makes a woman blest
Is by the farmer's wife possess'd.
Ye idle fair, who scorn employment,
Yours is a mimic pale enjoyment:
The royal treasures of content,
Unto the farmer's wife, are sent.

Ye maidens who are blest with sense,
Wit, beauty and intelligence;
Whene'er you leave the single life,
Be each, a thrifty farmer's wife.
Ye vainer ones, who're fond of show,
Who step so mincing as you go,
If you would make the best of life,
Be, (if you can) the farmer's wife.

16. "The Farmer's Wife" is given here in its entirety. Snow copied it into her journal, but it remained unpublished. See *Complete Poetry*, 20–22.

In 1828, Eliza encountered—and rejected—an attractive suitor. She mentions in her autobiography that "in my youth . . . without vanity [I] can say, I had what was considered very flattering proposals."[17] She does not give specifics, but James Barr Walker seems to be one example of that "very flattering" male interest. If a novelist were to write a historical novel based on Eliza's life, that novelist might feel the need to create a character like James Walker. But Walker—who printed Eliza's first published poems, sought her out at a dance, wrote her a love poem, and was finally spurned—was real. Best of all, he remembered Eliza and kept track of her life and career after she traveled west with the Saints. It is Walker, not Eliza, who tells us what happened. His good-natured account of this brief and apparently one-sided romantic episode was published as part of his memoirs more than fifty years later.

In 1828, Walker became half-owner and literary editor of the *Western Courier*. He wrote to "Angerona," one of the pen names Eliza used in her early poems, noting that some time had elapsed since Angerona had sent anything to the paper and inviting her to submit additional poems. Eliza's father soon arrived at the newspaper office to check on the man who had extended such an appreciative invitation to his daughter. "I had on a ruffled shirt that day," Walker writes, "and I did the amiable for the old gentleman in my blandest manner." Oliver Snow seemed to approve, and Eliza soon submitted another poem. Walker continues: "I had not yet seen the poetess but I was interested in the family, and wished to commend myself to their attention." He attended a dance that he knew Eliza would also attend, and he seems to have been favorably impressed.

But his courtship did not go well. "I offended the poetess unwittingly," Walker writes, "and I am not sure that she ever forgave me. I wrote a little scrap in verse, and inserted it in my paper." The poem begins

> *My love, the gift you gave me*
> *Has bound me in a spell,*

---

17. Snow, "Sketch," in Beecher, *Personal Writings,* 16.

As pleasing as the witcheries
Of which old fables tell.

The final line of the poem referred to Eliza as "My own delicious maid."[18]

Walker was right; he had indeed offended the poetess. She certainly was not his "own delicious maid"! Eliza apparently considered him an indiscriminate flirt. She immediately responded with a poem of her own, which, needless to say, marked the end of any possible romance. Walker boldly published Eliza's reply in his paper:

Say who on earth would not despise
The paltry thing which thousands share,
A friend in fractions! who would prize?
Or deem the piecemeal worth a care?[19]

But this rejected suitor apparently recovered from his disappointment. Within a few years, in fact, James Barr Walker had begun a career that would culminate in national recognition as an outstanding clergyman, theologian, and abolitionist. The life story and accomplishments of James Barr Walker can be found in many sources, including the *Dictionary of American Biography*. His best-known publication, still in print, is titled, amazingly, *The Philosophy of the Plan of Salvation*. It is impossible not to think what an outstanding couple Eliza R. Snow and James B. Walker would have made. But there was a purpose in her remaining single. Eliza herself, without naming Walker or any other prospective husband, later addressed the question of why she had remained unmarried for so many years:

"I remained single; and why, I could not comprehend at the time. But, when I embraced the fulness of the Gospel, in recalling the events of my past life, I felt, and

18. Reminiscences of James B. Walker are taken from his *Experiences of Pioneer Life in the Early Settlements and Cities of the West* (Chicago: Sumner and Co., 1881), 101–2, as are lines 1–4 from Walker's 16-line poem. See *Complete Poetry*, 1058–59.

19. Stanza 1 of "Say, Who on Earth," a 3-stanza poem published in *Western Courier*, March 7, 1829. See *Complete Poetry*, 27–28.

still feel to acknowledge the kind overruling hand in the providences of God in that circumstance, as fully as in any other in my mortal existence; I do not know that one of my former suitors have received the Gospel, which shows that I was singularly preserved from the bondage of a marriage tie which would, in all probability, have prevented my receiving, or from the free exercise of the religion which has been, and now is dearer to me than my life."[20]

We often think of Eliza R. Snow as such a through-and-through Latter-day Saint that it can be surprising to realize that there was, in fact, a pre-Mormon Eliza. All the poems and events we have been discussing occurred before her conversion to Mormonism; she had lived more than a third of her life before finally joining the Church in 1835, when she was thirty-one years old. Certainly the years between 1825 and 1835 were an eventful decade for Eliza. As we have seen, she attracted (and dismissed) at least one intelligent suitor; she launched her career as a published poet; and as a seeker of spiritual truth, she embraced the teachings of a prominent figure in American religion, Alexander Campbell. By the early months of 1828, she had firmly committed herself to New Testament Christianity as taught by Campbell. She was baptized according to these beliefs and joined other "restorationists" seeking unity through following the ancient or primitive order of Christian worship.

In February 1829, Eliza published a poem that remains something of a mystery. "Human Life—What Is It?" reflects many of the restorationist doctrines emphasized by Alexander Campbell, such as the ushering in of Christ's imminent millennial reign of peace by the "angel fly[ing] in the midst of heaven," as promised by John in Revelation 14:6. Eliza's image of an angel revealing "secret pages" (see stanzas 7 and 8) is almost certainly a reference to the angel of Revelation. Yet any Latter-day Saint, without knowing the poem's date of early 1829, would assume that the intriguing seventh and eighth stanzas of this poem refer to the angel Moroni and to the bringing forth of the Book of Mormon. Eliza herself had not at this time met Joseph Smith; it would be more than six years before she finally decided to be baptized a Latter-day

---

20. Snow, "Sketch," in Beecher, *Personal Writings*, 16.

Saint. Was she somehow inspired with a foreshadowing of truths that would one day be part of her life?[21]

Years later, after her baptism, Eliza copied the poem into her journal. She changed "secret pages" (the fifth stanza printed below) to "long-sealed pages," linking the poem explicitly to the Book of Mormon.

Human Life—What Is It?

I've seen the shadow passing by,
　When pass'd its being time was o'er—
I've seen the pointed arrow fly,
　'Twas found no more.

I've seen the tender, lovely flower
　Dismantled of its modest hue—
I've seen the pine majestic, tower
　And perish too.

Just such is life, 'tis but a dream,
　And all its scenes a trifling jest!
There's nought but Fancy's childish gleam
　To be possess'd.

But lo! a shining Seraph comes!
　Hark! 'tis the voice of sacred Truth;
He smiles, and on his visage blooms,
　Eternal youth.

He speaks of things before untold,
　Reveals what men nor angels knew,
The secret pages now unfold
　To human view.

Death's favored captives burst in twain,
　Their bond of union with the urn;
The lamp of life reviv'd again
　Will ever burn.

The Snows welcomed visitors to their home and encouraged open and lively discussion of politics and religion. Eliza described her parents as "free from bigotry and intolerance," her home as "a welcome resort for the honorable of all denominations."[22] In the early months of 1831, the Snow family's friend and minister, Sidney Rigdon, who was newly converted to the teachings of Joseph Smith, introduced them to the Prophet.

---

21. Lines 1–12 and 21–40 of "Human Life—What Is It?" a poem of 40 lines published in *Western Courier*, February 14, 1829. These are lines 1–4, 21–32, and 37–40. See *Complete Poetry*, 25–27.
22. Snow, "Sketch," in Beecher, *Personal Writings*, 8.

Leonora Snow Leavitt Morley.

Sometime during the winter of 1830–31, Joseph visited the Snow home. Eliza's oldest sister, Leonora, and their mother, Rosetta, responded immediately to the message of the restored gospel; they were baptized by Joseph Smith himself. Eliza, however, held back. Upon meeting Joseph, she "scrutinized his face closely" and acknowledged only that "his was an honest face."[23] We often read historical accounts of people who met Joseph Smith and recognized him immediately as a prophet of God, but Eliza was cautious.

Serious, prayerful study eventually led to her conversion. In 1835, four years after she first met Joseph Smith, she was touched by "the faith and humility of those who had received the gospel as taught by Joseph." "The spirit bore witness to me of the

---

23. Snow, "Sketch," in Beecher, *Personal Writings,* 9.

truth," she remembered. "My heart was now fixed; and I was baptized on the 5th of April, 1835."[24] She remained a devoted Latter-day Saint for the rest of her life.

On the evening following her baptism, Eliza received an unforgettable spiritual confirmation. "I realized the baptism of the Spirit," she said, "as sensibly as I did that of the water in the stream." She described the experience: "I saw a beautiful candle with an unusual long, bright blaze directly over my feet. I sought to know the interpretation, and received the following, 'The lamp of intelligence shall be lighted over your path.' I was satisfied."[25] This forward-looking promise seems to have been perfectly suited to Eliza and to the gifts that she would henceforth consecrate to the Church.

Eliza recalled that at some point during her four-year wait before deciding to enter the waters of baptism, "I prayed unto the Lord to let me know if the work were true, covenanting with him, if he did so, that I would ever praise his name in the congregation of the saints."[26] And praise him she did. Shortly after she was baptized, she wrote two hymn texts just in time for them to be included in the first Latter-day Saint hymnbook, Emma Smith's 1835 *A Collection of Sacred Hymns for the Church of the Latter Day Saints*. Both hymns are expressions of pure joy. The first one, set to a tune by Ebenezer Beesley that matches Eliza's text in its energetic delight, continues as part of Latter-day Saint hymnody today, under the title "Great Is the Lord."[27] The hymnal uses stanzas 1, 2, 5, and 6 of Eliza's poem.

Praise Ye the Lord

Great is the Lord: 'tis good to praise
His high and holy name:
Well may the saints in latter days
His wondrous love proclaim.

---

24. Snow, "Sketch," in Beecher, *Personal Writings*, 10.
25. Snow, "Sketch," in Beecher, *Personal Writings*, 10.
26. Cooperative Retrenchment Minutes, June 22, 1872, Church History Library, The Church of Jesus Christ of Latter-day Saints, Salt Lake City, Utah.
27. *Hymns* (1985), no. 77.

> The op'ning seals announce the day,
> By prophets long declar'd;
> When all, in one triumphant lay,
> Will join to praise the Lord.[28]

Eliza's second hymn rejoices in the Millennium. The eye of her poetic imagination sees rich details of the blessed time of Christ's Second Coming, with verdant landscapes, fragrant flowers, and lush vegetation. The Saints will not only share the companionship of angels but even walk with Christ himself.

The Glorious Day Is Rolling On

> The glorious day is rolling on—
> All glory to the Lord!
> When fair as at creation's dawn
> The earth will be restor'd.
>
> A perfect harvest then will crown
> The renovated soil;
> And rich abundance drop around,
> Without corroding toil:
>
> For Zion will like Eden bloom;
> And Jesus come to reign—
> The Saints immortal from the tomb
> With angels meet again.[29]

In these formative years, culminating with her baptism, Eliza arrived at a sense of her life's commitment as a poet: She would seek not worldly reputation but rather the

---

28. Stanzas from "Praise Ye the Lord." First published in *Messenger and Advocate,* August 1835, this text also appears on pages 92–93 of Emma Smith's *Collection of Sacred Hymns.* See *Complete Poetry,* 67–68.

29. Stanzas 1, 2, and 8 of "The Glorious Day Is Rolling On." Published in *Messenger and Advocate,* January 1836, this text also appears on pages 93–94 of Emma Smith's hymnal. See *Complete Poetry,* 69–70.

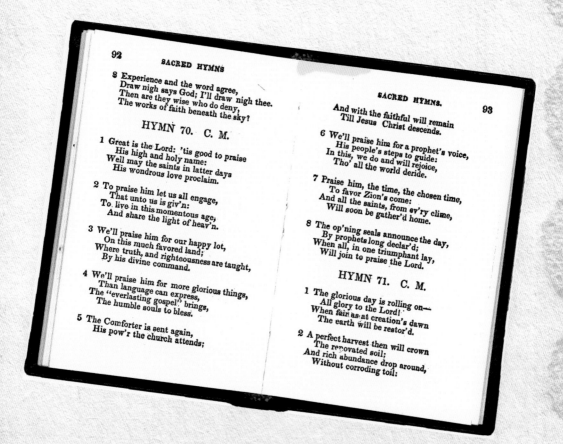

> 92   SACRED HYMNS
>
> 8 Experience and the word agree,
>   Draw nigh says God; I'll draw nigh thee.
>   Then are they wise who do deny,
>   The works of faith beneath the sky?
>
> HYMN 70.   C. M.
>
> 1 Great is the Lord: 'tis good to praise
>   His high and holy name:
>   Well may the saints in latter days
>   His wondrous love proclaim.
>
> 2 To praise him let us all engage,
>   That unto us is giv'n:
>   To live in this momentous age,
>   And share the light of heav'n.
>
> 3 We'll praise him for our happy lot,
>   On this much favored land;
>   Where truth, and righteousness are taught,
>   By his divine command.
>
> 4 We'll praise him for more glorious things,
>   Than language can express,
>   The "everlasting gospel" brings,
>   The humble souls to bless.
>
> 5 The Comforter is sent again,
>   His pow'r the church attends;

> SACRED HYMNS.   93
>
> And with the faithful will remain
> Till Jesus Christ descends.
>
> 6 We'll praise him for a prophet's voice,
>   His people's steps to guide:
>   In this, we do and will rejoice,
>   Tho' all the world deride.
>
> 7 Praise him, the time, the chosen time,
>   To favor Zion's come:
>   And all the saints, from ev'ry clime,
>   Will soon be gather'd home.
>
> 8 The op'ning seals announce the day,
>   By prophets long declar'd;
>   When all, in one triumphant lay,
>   Will join to praise the Lord.
>
> HYMN 71.   C. M.
>
> 1 The glorious day is rolling on—
>   All glory to the Lord!
>   When fair as at creation's dawn
>   The earth will be restor'd.
>
> 2 A perfect harvest then will crown
>   The renovated soil;
>   And rich abundance drop around,
>   Without corroding toil:

"nobler joys"[30] of service in the cause of spiritual truth. Nonetheless, as Eliza moved to Kirtland, Ohio, and began a new era of her life living among Latter-day Saints, she quickly discovered that those anticipated joys could be tempered by sorrows and hardships she could not have imagined.

---

30. A phrase from Snow's 32-line poem "The Better Choice," published in *Western Courier,* February 16, 1828. See *Complete Poetry,* 18–19.

ABOVE: *Two of Eliza's early hymn texts were included in Emma Smith's 1835 hymnal.*

Kirtland, Ohio, *by Glen Hopkinson. Eliza resided in Kirtland between 1836 and 1838 and then joined the Saints' migration to Missouri.*

AWAKE!

1836–1839

Eliza R. Snow did nothing by halves. She treasured the unfolding doctrines and revelations as taught by Joseph Smith, and her belief in his prophetic calling was firm. Her acceptance of the restored gospel of Jesus Christ would shape the rest of her life, determining not only her beliefs but her location, her associates, and her work. After her baptism, she would live with the Saints, suffer with them in their forced expulsions and resettlements, and dedicate her talents to their cause.

Under Joseph's direction in Kirtland, Ohio, a town only a few miles from Eliza's longtime family home in Mantua, Latter-day Saint converts steadily gathered to build homes and begin work on a temple. After her baptism in April 1835, Eliza remained at Mantua until the year's end; her younger sister Melissa died there in December. Eliza moved to Kirtland that month, boarding with Joseph and Emma Smith and teaching school, but she returned "at the close of the [spring] term"[1] to her parents' home in Mantua. It is probably accurate to say that Eliza's decision to relocate once and for all to Kirtland in January 1837 required her to begin to confront true adulthood for the first time in her life. After she "bade a final adieu to the home of my

---

1. Snow, "Sketch," in Beecher, *Personal Writings*, 10.

youth, to share the fortunes of the people of God,"[2] she was no longer the sheltered daughter in a long-established and comfortable Mantua home. She began a more independent life in Kirtland, one that was unfamiliar and yet anchored by the new faith she had embraced.

How did Eliza's conversion affect her poetry? A look at how she signed her poems, before and after her conversion, helps to answer this question. During the years before her baptism, Eliza had used a series of pen names, concealing her identity under such fictional identities as Angerona, Pocahontas, and Tullia. Pseudonyms can be a form of modesty, a way of declining credit and recognition for a poem, but of course they also can be a way of escaping responsibility. Eliza's first two hymn texts mark a major turning point in her poetic career, symbolized by a bold decision: She signed these hymn texts with her own name and thereafter took ownership of all the poems she wrote for the rest of her life.

The abandonment of pen names was part of her decision to consecrate her poetic gifts to the cause of the gospel. Several years later, in a poem she wrote to a fellow poet, she described her decision to acknowledge her authorship and speak out courageously, without the mask of a pseudonym, on behalf of her beliefs:

> *When young in years—in all a child—*
> *With thought untrain'd, and fancy wild*
> *'Twas my delight to spend an hour*
> *Beneath the Muse's fav'rite bow'r;*
> *While then I fan'd Parnassus' fire*
> *The letter'd pinions ask'd my lyre;*
> *I deeply scorn'd the Poet's fame*
> *And from the world witheld my name.*
>
> *But when from the eternal throne,*
> *The truth of God around me shone;*

2. Snow, "Sketch," in Beecher, *Personal Writings,* 10.

Its glories my affections drew
And soon I tun'd my harp anew:
By counsel which I'd fain abide
I laid fictitious names aside:
My duty, not a love of fame
Induc'd me to divulge my name.

It surely is a glorious thing
To mount imagination's wing;
With Inspiration's chart unfurl'd
That bids defiance to the world;
And ride triumphantly abroad
Where the unthinking never trod,
And gain an empire for the mind
That leaves tradition's throne behind.[3]

During 1836 and 1837, nearly all of Eliza's family moved to Kirtland, including her older sister, Leonora, her parents, Oliver and Rosetta Snow, and their two youngest sons. Eliza recalled that "I . . . was happy in an association with the Saints, fully appreciating their enlarged views and rich intelligence from the fountain of Eternal Truth, through the inspiration of the Most High; and was present on the ever memorable occasion of the Dedication of the Kirtland Temple. . . . In that Temple, after its dedication, I witnessed many manifestations of the power of God." Her testimony of Joseph Smith continued to increase during this time: "[I] had ample opportunity to mark his 'daily walk and conversation,' as a prophet of God; and the more I became acquainted with him, the more I appreciated him as such. His lips ever flowed with instruction and kindness."[4]

---

3. Lines 33–56 of "Lines Addressed to Mr. Huelett," a 56-line poem dated August 28, 1843. Snow copied the poem into her diary, but it was not published. See *Complete Poetry*, 258–60.

4. Snow, "Sketch," in Beecher, *Personal Writings*, 10–11.

As she would do again in Nauvoo, Eliza taught school in Kirtland. In the spring of 1836, she was employed at "a select school for young ladies"[5] while boarding with the Prophet's family. She again "resided in the family of Joseph Smith, and taught his family school"[6] when she returned to settle in Kirtland in 1837.

Along with consecrating her talents to the cause of the restored gospel, Eliza consecrated her means. When she moved out of her parents' home, they gave her inheritance to her, and she chose to donate it to the building of the Kirtland Temple. "I went into the united order and all I possessed went in," she recalled many years later in speaking to the Relief Society in Brigham City. "I had money; I sent for the building committee of the Kirtland Temple[,] asked if they wanted money[;] they felt very thankful."[7]

Eliza's younger brother Lorenzo, a student at Oberlin College and not yet a Latter-day Saint, wrote to her on March 12, 1836, "I am delighted in learning that you enjoy so much happiness in Kirtland."[8] A short time later, at Eliza's invitation, Lorenzo visited Kirtland, where he joined with Joseph Smith and other Church leaders in the study of Hebrew at the School of the Prophets. "While studying a dead language," Eliza wrote later, "he also studied the eternal principles of a living faith."[9] He was baptized in June 1836. This beloved brother eventually became an apostle and, in 1898, was sustained as the fifth president of the Church. Eliza's and Lorenzo's devotion to each other and their shared testimony were enduring joys in the lives of both.

The Snows did not stay long in Kirtland, however. As the Latter-day Saints' increasing political power in the township rankled longtime residents, and as Church

---

5. Box Elder Stake Relief Society Minutes, 1868–1876, 1875–1884, September 10, 1878, Church History Library, The Church of Jesus Christ of Latter-day Saints, Salt Lake City, Utah; hereafter cited as Church History Library.

6. Lorenzo Snow to Eliza R. Snow, March 12, 1836, Lorenzo Snow Journal and Letterbook, 1836–45, Church History Library.

7. Box Elder Stake Relief Society Minutes, 1868–1876, 1875–1884, September 10, 1878, Church History Library.

8. Snow to Snow, March 12, 1836.

9. Snow, "Sketch," in Beecher, *Personal Writings,* 11.

Lorenzo Snow.

leaders' failed attempt to operate a bank worsened rather than eased the city's economic distress, the community quickly unraveled. Eliza later described the apostasy that tore the community apart:

> *For see, ah, see! in yonder eastern land—*
> *In Kirtland City, a promiscuous band,*
> *Where wheat and tares to such a height had grown*
> *That Saints could scarce from hypocrites be known!*[10]

In January 1838, pressed from both outside and within the Church, the Prophet and other leaders fled for their lives to Missouri. The Snows were among

---

10. Lines 81–84 of "The Gathering of the Saints, and the Commencement of the City of Adam-ondi-Ahman," a poem of 198 lines first published in Snow's *Poems* (1856). See *Complete Poetry*, 78–84.

approximately sixteen hundred Saints who migrated to northern Missouri, settling initially in Daviess County. In July 1838, Oliver Snow purchased fertile land and a "double log house" at Adam-ondi-Ahman. In May 1838, Joseph Smith had given the settlement this name, meaning "the place where Adam shall come to visit his people, or the Ancient of Days shall sit."[11] It was sacred ground.

In traveling from Ohio to Missouri and later from Missouri to Illinois, Eliza encountered vast grasslands that were very different from the dense woods of her native Ohio. When she had earlier heard travelers describe the beauty of the prairie, she had not believed these descriptions:

> *I grew incredulous that Nature's dress*
> *Should be so rich, and so domestic, and*
> *So beautiful, without the touch of Art;*
> *And thought the picture fancifully wrought.*

These lines are from a poem often cited as one of her finest, titled "My First View of a Western Prairie." Her first glimpse of the magnificent open grasslands was "As if awaking from a nightly dream, / Into a scenery grand and strangely new":

> *Amaz'd, I view'd until my optic nerve*
> *Grew dull and giddy with the phrenzy of*
> *The innocent delight; and I exclaim'd*
> *With Sheba's queen, "one half had not been told."[12]*

When we read this poem, we are convinced of what she claims in its opening lines: "The loveliness of Nature, always did /Delight me."[13]

---

11. See Doctrine and Covenants 116.

12. See 1 Kings 10:7.

13. Lines 22–25, 29–30, 56–59, and 1–2 of the 74-line poem "My First View of a Western Prairie," published in *Quincy Whig*, June 29, 1839. See *Complete Poetry*, 91–94.

Saints being driven from Jackson County, Missouri, in 1833,
as depicted by artist C. C. A. Christensen.

Latter-day Saints found good land but experienced no peace in their new Missouri settlements. Clashing beliefs and interests bred conflict between the newcomers and other settlers. Some twenty-eight years after she left Missouri, when Eliza began to direct much of her writing and publishing activity toward Latter-day Saint children, she wrote an article for the *Juvenile Instructor* describing the Missouri hardships. Knowing that she was writing for a young audience, she chose a conversational tone, with simple words and sentences. She did not try to summarize the long and complex story of the Missouri persecutions. Instead, she selected one sad incident that she knew would touch the hearts of young people and linger in their memory:

Our Dog Jack

We had a very large watch-dog, which my father took with him from Ohio, on purpose to guard the wagons while we were traveling. As soon as my brother Lorenzo [who had been very ill] was strong enough to walk out, and carry a rifle, he amused himself by hunting turkeys, which were very abundant in that part of Missouri.

Missouri Crossing, *by Glen Hopkinson. In bitterly cold weather, Eliza and her family fled Missouri and began the journey that would take them to Nauvoo.*

Whenever he went on those little hunting excursions, the watch-dog, Jack, was sure to accompany him. Some dogs seem quite sensible, as my young readers will understand, and Jack was uncommonly smart, and seemed to realize that his master had but little strength—he would walk as stilly as possible, at my brother's heels, until they came in sight of game, when he would place himself directly in front, and raise his head sufficiently, then hold his head perfectly still for his master to rest the rifle on his head, to shoot.

. . . Jack was highly prized by all the family, and although a dog, he was worthy of respect, because he was a true friend. . . . We had learned that Jack could be trusted, and when we knew that we were surrounded by mobocrats, we could lie down at night, feeling pretty safe, knowing that no one could approach the house, until the faithful dog had given the alarm.

   I think by this time, my little friends are feeling enough interest for the dog Jack, to wish to know what became of him. I will tell you. Our Missouri neighbors (if I may call those neighbors who were plotting our destruction) saw that Jack was true to us, and they were afraid of him, and tried to entice him away, but when they found it impossible to coax him to leave us, they shot him. We all felt very sorry to lose poor Jack, and two of my younger brothers dug a grave and buried him with all the formalities that the occasion called for, and, with great childish lamentations, pronounced him a martyr.[14]

As the number of Latter-day Saints in the region rapidly increased, violent exchanges between zealous Mormons and hostile Missourians escalated until, at the end of October 1838, Missouri's governor mandated the expulsion of Mormons from the state by the following spring. In December 1838, the Snows relinquished their new house in Adam-ondi-Ahman and escaped threatening Missouri vigilantes by fleeing some forty miles south to the Saints' headquarters settlement at Far West, Caldwell County, Missouri. "Subservient to [the governor's] order," Eliza recalled, "a posse of Militia was to remain in the vicinity, ostensibly to protect the Saints; but we could not decide which was the most to be dreaded[,] the Militia or the mob—no property was safe within the reach of either."[15]

Eliza long remembered their flight in the harsh December weather. After they had traveled about two miles, she recalled in her brief "Sketch of My Life," she was walking alone ahead of the wagons "to warm my aching feet" when she "met one of the so-called Militia who accosted me with 'Well, I think this will cure you of your faith.' Looking him squarely in the eye, I replied, 'No, Sir, it will take more than this to cure

14. Snow, "Little Incidents for Little Readers," *Juvenile Instructor,* November 15, 1866, 2.
15. Snow, "Sketch," in Beecher, *Personal Writings,* 12.

me of my faith.' His countenance dropped, and he responded, 'I must confess you are a better soldier than I am.' I passed on, thinking that, unless he was above the average of his fellows in that section, I was not complimented by his confession."[16]

On the first night of this bitterly cold journey, about eighty Mormon refugees found what shelter they could in a log structure so small that most of them had to sit or stand all night, rather than being able to lie down. Eliza and her sister "managed so that mother lay down, and we sat by (on the floor, of course), to prevent her being trampled on, for the crowd was such that people were hardly responsible for their movements."[17] Eliza's mother suffered from poor health prior to her death in 1846, and Eliza always considered her to be a martyr to the persecutions of Missouri.

In remembering the intense discomfort of that night in the crowded and inadequate shelter, however, Eliza recalled that resolute cheerfulness could triumph over adversity: "The cold was so intense that, in spite of well packing, our food was frozen hard, bread and all, and although a blazing fire was burning on one side of the room, we could not get to it to thaw our suppers. . . . But, withal, that was a very merry night. None but saints can be happy under every circumstance. . . . Not a complaint was heard—all were cheerful, and judging from appearances, strangers would have taken us to be pleasure excursionists rather than a band of gubernatorial exiles."[18]

"Much, much is learned by contrast," Eliza later wrote.[19] Contrast marked her first years as a Latter-day Saint in Ohio and Missouri. A desire to be useful propelled her through dire circumstances and energized her in better times. She filled her days with a varied rhythm of tasks. She wrote letters; in Kirtland, she taught school; she hungrily studied the restored gospel; she nursed sick family members and friends. For the often uprooted Saints, times of relative ease might be followed by a struggle to secure the basic necessities of life. Most clothes were made by hand, and Eliza was never

---

16. Snow, "Sketch," in Beecher, *Personal Writings,* 12.

17. Snow, "Sketch," in Beecher, *Personal Writings,* 13.

18. Snow, "Sketch," in Beecher, *Personal Writings,* 13–14.

19. Line 21 of the 52-line poem "Contrast." See *Complete Poetry,* 472–74.

idle as a needlewoman. She made caps, collars, and any needed article of clothing, including, George A. Smith noted, "a pair of pantaloons"[20] for him to take with him when he left on his mission in 1838. In one emergency, her needlework helped obtain cornmeal. She tells us that in Far West "a spirit of mobocracy was boldly manifested by leading citizens in the county opposing the Latter-day Saints." The Missourians prevented the Saints from obtaining flour by "laying an embargo on all of the flouring mills in that section, and preventing our people from obtaining breadstuff. Our father had abundance of wheat, but could get no grinding. In this dilemma we had to resort to graters, made by perforating tin pails and stovepipes, on which we grated corn for bread material. . . . Elder Abel Butterfield, Lorenzo's traveling [missionary] companion, was stopping with us, while waiting for my brother to regain his strength sufficient for travel, and as he required clothing made, previous to departure, my sister proposed to join me in doing his needle work, tailoring, etc., if he would give his time in grating meal for the family, which he gladly accepted."[21]

In terms of Eliza's poetry, the nearly three-year period from January 1836 to October 1838 presents something of a mystery. Conflict in Kirtland, the subsequent move to different locations in the state of Missouri, and the traumatic lawlessness she encountered there seem to have silenced her poetic voice. No poems from this period, published or unpublished, have yet been located; for these three years, she left her lyre "unstrung" while she wrestled with discouragement. She did not at any point in her life specifically discuss the reasons for this withdrawal from poetry-writing, but whatever the causes, her creative fires had temporarily gone out.

In an undated and unpublished poem, one of the most personal she ever wrote and one of the few instances in which she admits to despair and weariness, she described her inability to awaken the "chords" of her poetic lyre:

20. Jarvis, *George A. Smith Family*, 59.
21. Snow, *Biography and Family Record*, 41–42.

On Being Importun'd by a Friend, to Write

You ask me to awake its chords again—
But dull monotonies would fill the strain
For every strain has been twice sung,
And every chorus, three times rung,
And every novelty has grown insane.

I would not aim at things, before unsung,
Nor such as move upon a seraph's tongue,
But, till its numbers shall be fraught
With novel sound and native thought,
O, let my stupid lyre remain unstrung.[22]

These are words of depression and utter discouragement, painful to read. Yet, as if we were reading the journal of a beloved grandmother who had frankly recorded the difficult experiences in her life, we are grateful for the honesty. Without such openness, we might believe, wrongly, that a faithful person never encounters times of struggle. And Eliza's poem presents a wonderful paradox: her poem about *not* being able to write a poem is one of the finest and most moving ever to come from her pen.

The "Friend" referred to in the title of this poem may well have been the Prophet Joseph Smith. Sometime in the early fall of 1838, in response to Eliza's need or the Church's need or both, Joseph Smith appointed her to speak through her poems to and on behalf of the Latter-day Saints. Joseph's invitation was not for a single poem to commemorate a person or event but for her to resume composing sacred poetry. The establishment of Zion, a community of sanctified Saints, required the consecrated talents of everyone. Eliza was now called upon to consecrate her special gift, obvious from the two celebratory poems she had composed in 1835, and help build the

---

22. Lines 6–15 of a 15-line poem. See *Complete Poetry*, 77.

OPPOSITE: *Eliza's handkerchief and a poem from her journal in which she responds to an unnamed friend's request for her to resume writing sacred poetry.*

On being importun'd by a Friend, to write.

Friendship's imperative — I own its sway:
Its unction, angels dare not disobey;
    And could its sacred voice inspire
    Sweet pathos through my slumb'ring lyre,
To you I'd dedicate its softest lay.

You ask me to awake its chords again —
But dull monotonies would fill the strain
    For every strain has been twice sung,
    And every chorus, thrice times rung,
And every novelty has grown insane.

I would not aim at things, before unsung,
Nor such as move upon a seraph's tongue,
    But, till its numbers shall be fraught
    With novel sound and native thought,
O, let my stupid lyre remain unstrung.

kingdom through her verse. Her close friend and colleague Emmeline B. Wells reported that Eliza "was designated by Joseph Smith the Prophet, 'Zion's Poetess.'"[23] Though the title was not actually attached to Eliza until much later, in the 1850s, the calling almost certainly came in Missouri. It crystallized her sense of vocation as a poet.

"Awake!" That was the first word of the poem with which Eliza finally broke her three-year silence in October 1838. She once again summoned her poetic inspiration, her "slumbering Minstrel," and with words of shock and indignation she decried the betrayal of government officials, proclaiming that they had failed to protect the lives and property of the Saints. The poem of almost 200 lines is a courageous, confident declaration of renewed poetic commitment:

> *Awake! my slumbering Minstrel; thou hast lain*
> *Like one that's number'd with th' unheeded slain!*
> *Unlock thy music—let thy numbers flow*
> *Like torrents bursting from the melting snow.*

As she continued, Eliza used strong language to describe the terrible scenes of persecution and suffering in Missouri:

> *'Twas Autumn: Summer's melting breath was gone,*
> *And Winter's gelid blast was stealing on:*
> *To meet its dread approach, with anxious care*
> *The houseless Saints were struggling to prepare;*
> *When round about a desp'rate mob arose,*
> *Like tigers waking from a night's repose—*
> *They come like hordes from nether shades let loose—*
> *Men without hearts—just made for Satan's use!*
> *With wild, demoniac rage they sally forth,*
> *Resolv'd to drive the Saints of God from earth.*

---

23. "Eliza Roxie Snow Smith: A Tribute of Affection," *Woman's Exponent* 16 (December 15, 1887): 109.

This is the angry Eliza, the one who is indignant—as she continued to be throughout her life—that in her beloved America such wrongdoing and persecution could be allowed. Three days after she wrote these lines, in fact, Missouri governor Lilburn W. Boggs issued the Extermination Order, mandating that Latter-day Saints leave the state by the following spring. Near the end of the poem, however, are lines that express her confidence in the divine destiny of the Saints as the Lord's covenant people:

> *Well may the nations of the earth give ear,*
> *For lo! The kingdom of our God is near.*
> *Let proud usurpers lay their ensigns down,*
> *And haughty tyrants lightly hold the crown!*
> *All rival monarchies must soon give way,*
> *And Heaven's eternal kingdom bear the sway.*[24]

Pen belonging to Eliza R. Snow. The poem, from her journal, is "The Tree of Life."

---

24. Lines 1–4, 117–26, and 181–86 of "The Gathering of the Saints," a poem of 198 lines. Written in October 1838, it was first published in *Poems* (1856). See *Complete Poetry*, 78–84.

Across the next four decades, Eliza wrote dozens of poems for friends and acquaintances, some of them bidding welcome or farewell, some offering sympathy in times of sorrow, and some conveying humor and good cheer. Yet she was committed to the public role of a poet. In using her poetic gifts to build the Saints' latter-day Zion, she was inspired by serious literary traditions, including the writings of the prophets and seers of the Old Testament. In addition, she admired such seventeenth- and eighteenth-century poets as Alexander Pope and Philip Freneau, who often used poetry for political purposes as a means of public debate and rebuke.

The privations and injustices that plagued the Saints in Ohio and Missouri provoked Eliza to write a steady stream of poems that express her anger against their oppressors. On October 30, 1838, three days after Governor Boggs issued the Extermination Order, approximately two hundred armed men violated a truce by attacking the Mormon settlement at Jacob Hawn's mill on Shoal Creek, Caldwell County. The mob surrounded the shop, killing seventeen Mormons and wounding fourteen others. Eliza chronicled this awful event in a poem called "The Slaughter on Shoal Creek":

> *Ye wives and mothers; think of women then*
> *Left in a group of dead, and dying men,*
> *Her hopes were blasted—all her prospects riv'n*
> *Save one; she trusted in the God of heav'n,*
> *Long, for the dead, her widow'd heart will crave*
> *A last kind office—yes, a DECENT GRAVE!*[25]

On March 5, 1839, Eliza and her family joined the Saints' forced exodus from Caldwell County, Missouri. Only two weeks earlier, she had expressed her unflagging commitment and determined optimism in a letter to a friend:

> It astonishes our enemies that our people *suffer* no more while
> passing thro' these scenes of *suffering*. They say, the Mormons have

---

25. Lines 31–36 of the 40-line poem "The Slaughter on Shoal Creek." See *Complete Poetry*, 103–5.

Quincy, Illinois, about 1859.

always rejoic'd in tribulation, but they [the enemies] will do something now that they [the Saints] will not rejoice in. . . . They have not burnt any of us at the stake *yet,*—they have imprison'd, whip'd, ston'd and shot some but *death* does not terrify us enough to suit them, for they say that the Mormons are so d—d sure of going to heaven, they had as lief die as not. The Lord maketh the wrath of man to praise him [see Psalm 76:10]. Let *his* name be magnified.[26]

Oliver and Rosetta Snow and their two sons moved to northern Illinois, but Eliza and her sister Leonora stopped farther south at Quincy for a short time, where Eliza wrote some twenty poems that were published in the Quincy *Whig* newspaper. In one of these poems, titled "To the Citizens of Quincy," she expressed "Pure Gratitude, our free-will off'ring" to the townspeople for receiving the outcast Saints with such kindness:

> *Ye Sons and Daughters of Benevolence,*
> *Whose hearts are tun'd to notes of sympathy*

---

26. Eliza R. Snow to "Esqr. Streator," Caldwell County, Missouri, February 22, 1839, Western Reserve Historical Society, Cleveland, Ohio.

> *Who have put forth your liberal hand to meet*
> *The urgent wants of the oppress'd and poor![27]*

During the next three years Eliza published more than forty poems. Her poetic energies and inspiration had surely returned. Now, without interruption, she would chronicle her people's history, broadcast their beliefs, and speak in their defense. Her works were beginning to be recognized, she later recalled, as "productions from the pen of a <u>Mormon girl</u>."[28] Eliza R. Snow had assumed a new and enduring role as a distinctively Mormon poet.

Eliza arrived in Illinois in March 1839. Throughout her life, she often wrote an introspective poem as each year came to a close, and many of these "annual reviews" were full of praise and gratitude. But with all the disorder, uncertainty, and frustration that 1839 had brought, it is no surprise that she found it difficult to be reconciled to the uprooting and mistreatment of the Saints. A wistful sense of loss pervades "The Year Has Gone," written on January 1, 1840. Even poetry seems destined for extinction:

> *The year has gone, and with it fled*
> *The schemes of many an aching head;*
>> *The half-formed schemes,*
>> *Like fairy dreams,*
>> *Which take their flight*
>> *Before the light,*
> *Or perish in the noon-day beams.*
>
> *The year has gone, and with it flown*
> *The sage's thought—the songster's tone—*
>> *Gone to pervade*
>> *Oblivion's shade:*

---

27. Lines 44 and 1–4 of "To the Citizens of Quincy," a poem of 59 lines. See *Complete Poetry*, 86–88.
28. Snow, "Sketch," in Beecher, *Personal Writings*, 15; underlining in original.

And with them dies
No more to rise,
The product of the Poet's head.[29]

But her arrival in Illinois must have given her hope. The Saints were confident that they had found a refuge. Their Prophet, finally released from prison after almost six months of confinement, had joined them. They soon named their new city Nauvoo. As the days and weeks went by, the new converts, new buildings, and the spiritual guidance of Joseph Smith promised better, more peaceful days ahead.

---

29. Lines 29–42 of a 42-line poem. See *Complete Poetry,* 105–7.

Nauvoo, Illinois, 1859, *by John Schroder. From almost nothing, Eliza and her fellow Saints, under the leadership of Joseph Smith, built a thriving city on the banks of the Mississippi River.*

Chapter Three

NAUVOO, THE BEAUTIFUL

1839–1845

How Eliza loved Nauvoo! "'Tis the place of all others most dear," she wrote in 1841.[1] She rejoiced in the promise and beauty of the city that was beginning to rise around her. "[This location] seemed to have been held in reserve to meet the occasion, for none but Saints full of faith, and trusting in the power of God, could have established that city," she wrote later. "To narrate what transpired within the seven years, in which we built and occupied Nauvoo, the beautiful, would fill many volumes. . . . Some of the most important events of my life transpired within that brief term."[2]

Founded by Joseph Smith on an unpromising Mississippi riverbank in Illinois, the city provided a refuge for the beleaguered Saints. During the next seven years, thousands of Latter-day Saints from the United States, Canada, and Great Britain flocked to Nauvoo in order to be near the Prophet Joseph Smith. In Nauvoo, civic and religious life were one. United by their belief in Joseph Smith and the latter-day restoration of the gospel, they were determined to be a holy people. A temple was begun, with Joseph Smith declaring that new truths would be revealed within the House of the Lord rising on the hill. One of Eliza's poems expressed the pride of the

---

1. "Farewell to the Country," *Quincy Whig,* June 26, 1841. See *Complete Poetry,* 158–59.
2. Snow, "Sketch," in Beecher, *Personal Writings,* 16.

community of Saints in their growing city, with its attractive public buildings and its energizing sense of divine purpose:

> *There the city's heart rejoices—*
> *Business with her thousand voices,*
> *With improvement steps apace:*
> *Architecture is unfolding,*
> *Specimens of richest moulding,*
> *Rising up with lofty grace.*[3]

Eliza had joined the exodus to Illinois in 1839, when the clashes with antagonistic neighbors in Missouri and a gubernatorial evacuation order left the Saints no choice but to flee the state. She had endured threats and hostility in Ohio and Missouri and remained loyal and faithful. Even in the relative peace of Nauvoo, however, Eliza's existence was still somewhat precarious. She moved from home to home and worked as a schoolteacher and seamstress, leaving behind the family solidarity and stability that characterized her childhood and young womanhood in Ohio. Yet in spite of these uncertainties, Eliza wrote some of her finest poems while in Nauvoo, including three hymn texts that are still part of Latter-day Saint hymnody today: "Though Deepening Trials," "Awake, Ye Saints of God," and "O My Father."[4]

Eliza's reputation as a writer was one reason she was invited to draft the constitution for a "ladies society," an initiative that led to the organization of the Female Relief Society of Nauvoo under the direction of Joseph Smith. On March 17, 1842, at the founding meeting of the new society, with twenty members present, Eliza was elected secretary. She meticulously recorded minutes of the first year's meetings, including the six sermons Joseph Smith delivered to the Relief Society. She carried the

---

3. Lines 19–24 of "Ode to Spring," a 30-line poem published in *Times and Seasons,* May 15, 1843. See *Complete Poetry,* 241–42.

4. *Hymns* (1985), nos. 122, 17, and 292, respectively. For their original titles, texts, and dates, see *Complete Poetry,* 130–33 and 312–14.

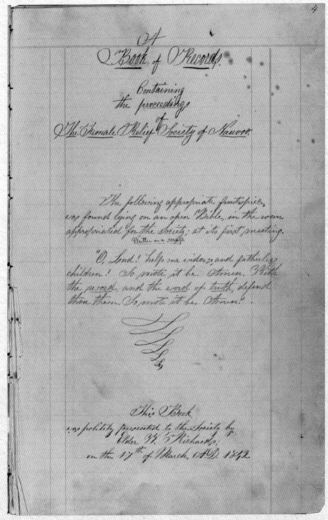

Title Page of Nauvoo Relief Society Minute Book,
created by Eliza R. Snow.

1842–44 minute book with her to the West, and she preserved the volume and shared its contents with her sisters until her death.[5] "You see by these minutes, that Joseph Smith said if the sisters would carry out his counsel, they would become the most

5. This volume, Nauvoo Relief Society Minutes, 1842–1844, is in Church History Library, The Church of Jesus Christ of Latter-day Saints, Salt Lake City, Utah; hereafter cited as Church History Library.

glorious organization that had ever been," she told women in Draper, Utah, in 1870.[6] Eliza was a woman of vision; did she, like the Prophet, foresee that this organization would one day number its members in the millions around the world?

As society membership increased during the spring and summer of 1842, Eliza published a poem describing the group's purposes. Although some of Eliza's phrasing may sound a little old-fashioned today, her poem resonates as clearly with the aims and commitments of today's Relief Society as it did with the Relief Society of 1842.

The Female Relief Society of Nauvoo
What Is It?

It is an Institution form'd to bless
The poor, the widow, and the fatherless—
To clothe the naked and the hungry feed,
And in the holy paths of virtue, lead.

To seek out sorrow, grief and mute despair,
And light the lamp of hope eternal there—
To try the strength of consolation's art
By breathing comfort to the mourning heart.

It is an Order, *fitted and design'd*
To meet the wants of body, and of mind—
To seek the wretched, in their lone abode—
Supply their wants, and raise their hearts to God.[7]

Eliza's years in Nauvoo gave her an opportunity to deepen her testimony of the restored gospel and to continue to learn from the Prophet Joseph Smith. "His expansive mind grasped the great plan of salvation and solved the mystic problem of man's

---

6. Draper Ward, East Jordan Stake, Relief Society Minutes, May 26, 1870, Church History Library.
7. Lines 1–8 and 21–24 of a 24-line poem published in *Times and Seasons,* July 1, 1842. See *Complete Poetry,* 204–5.

Joseph Smith.

destiny," she later wrote.[8] She testified that Joseph was a prophet of God who taught by divine revelation the character of God and His relationship to humanity. The premortal existence, the holy priesthood, celestial marriage, and temple ordinances for the living and for the dead were all elements of a comprehensive theology that extended to exalt and redeem the faithful daughters and sons of God.

Among Eliza's many poetic tributes to Joseph was "Two Chapters of the Life of President Joseph Smith," a poem of 301 lines proclaiming his prophetic calling and the importance of his ministry. In this poem, Eliza described with deep reverence the young Joseph's vision of God the Father and His Son Jesus Christ, the event that opened the heavens and commenced the restoration of the gospel in the latter days.

---

8. Snow, "Sketch," in Beecher, *Personal Writings,* 11.

Eliza took no liberties with the events of this sacred narrative; she followed closely Joseph Smith's own description of this experience in the account included today in the Pearl of Great Price as Joseph Smith–History 1:11–20.[9] She did, however, add a rich and touching poetic layer to this story. Always careful in her choice of an appropriate poetic meter for various subjects, she wrote this poem in blank verse, the line-pattern that was the favorite of Shakespeare, Milton, and other great English-language poets that Eliza knew through her own reading. Blank verse consists of unrhymed ten-syllable lines, with the stress falling on the even-numbered syllables. Eliza even fit quotations from scripture skillfully into this pattern; for example, she rephrases "If any of you lack wisdom, let him ask" (James 1:5) as "If any man lack wisdom, let him ask," a perfect line of blank verse. The lofty and respectful tone of the poem perfectly suits the retelling of this all-important story, heightening the suspense and drama moment by moment. Here is the excerpt that describes the First Vision:

> *He sought retirement in the woodland shade;*
> *In secret there to lift his heart and voice*
> *To God, in prayer. In all his life before,*
> *He had not shap'd his thoughts and his desires*
> *For vocal supplication. In the depth*
> *Of nature's wild retreat—where secrecies*
> *Of thought pour'd forth, could only reach the ear*
> *Of Him to whom the secrets of all hearts*
> *Are known—he spread the burthen of his soul*
> *Before the Lord. He scarce had bow'd himself*
> *In humble posture, when, with iron grasp,*
> *A power invisible laid hold on him.*
> *His prayer was interrupted, for his tongue*
> *Was suddenly in speechless silence chain'd.*

---

9. Joseph Smith recorded the experience. For the 1838–1841 manuscript documents that became this scripture, see Davidson et al., *Histories,* 1:204–14.

Thick atmospheric darkness gather'd round—
Destruction seem'd inevitable, and
Into the deep recesses of his heart
Despair was fastening its poison'd barb.
Then, with a mighty effort of his mind,
He rais'd his struggling heart to God, and sought
Deliverance from above; when suddenly
A pillar, brighter than the noon-day sun,
Precisely o'er his head, descending, fell
Around him. . . .

                                    . . . And were
The glorious figures which he saw, the forms
Of airiness and wild delusive thought?
O no: the heavens had verily upfurl'd
The sable curtain which defines the bounds
'Twixt earth and immortality; and he
Was gazing on celestials, and he heard
The voice of the Eternal.

                              One of the
Bright personages whom he saw, referr'd
Him to the other, and address'd him thus,
"Joseph, this is my well beloved Son,
Hear him."

In concluding the poem, Eliza bore witness that young Joseph had felt "The power of the Eternal Deity" and "The bulwark of the favor of the Lord."[10]

While in Kirtland, Latter-day Saints had begun to learn of the importance of temples. Eliza had attended the dedication of the Kirtland Temple and witnessed

---

10. Lines 167, 177–200, 216–28, 290, and 301 of a 301-line poem first published in its entirety in Snow's *Poems* (1856). See *Complete Poetry*, 248–58.

The Nauvoo Temple, *by C. C. A. Christensen.*

miraculous events at that time. As a new temple began to rise in Nauvoo, with the summer and fall of 1841 being particularly productive for the construction, Eliza and her fellow Saints looked forward once again to the promised blessings of the temple. She wrote the first of several temple anthems in 1841. Here is an excerpt from the sixty-line poem:

Lo, the Savior is coming, the prophets declare—
The times are fulfilling; O Zion, prepare!
The Savior is coming: but where shall he come?
Will he find in the palace of princes, a home?
No! O no, in his temple he'll surely attend;
But O where, is the "temple," where Christ shall descend?
Oh, ye Saints, be admonish'd by Time's rolling car;
It is rapidly onward! Hear, ye from afar!

Come, and bring in your treasures—your wealth from abroad:
Come, and build up the city and Temple of God. [11]

Eliza received the ordinance of the endowment in Nauvoo in December 1845, and she would later write, "Much of the winter of 1845–6, I spent officiating in the Temple—the upper part of which was sufficiently completed for administering the sacred ordinances of the holy Priesthood as God had revealed them."[12]

As was typical for a single woman of that time, Eliza moved from one household to another during her seven years in and around Nauvoo, sometimes living with family, sometimes with friends, and sometimes with people she did not know well. She continued to be employed as a seamstress and taught school while boarding in the homes of Sidney Rigdon and Joseph Smith. In the course of these many relocations, she must have longed for some privacy and solitude. When she wrote a poem called "Retirement," transcribed into her diary but unpublished during her lifetime, she was living in Joseph and Emma Smith's home, probably the overcrowded old homestead, where privacy was at a minimum. Seven people, in addition to guests and short-term boarders, may have shared the four-room house. Most of Eliza's poems reflect a public voice, but this one is a refreshingly personal description of the blessings of solitude.[13]

Eliza dearly loved her parents and her brothers and sisters, and she often paid tribute to her family and to the happiness of their life together. She maintained close ties with her sister Leonora, and the two of them, with Leonora's two young daughters, lived together for some time near Lima, Illinois. And always close to her heart was her faithful brother Lorenzo, who would one day become president of the Church. He served a highly successful mission in England from May 1840 to April 1843. When he returned to Nauvoo, Eliza waited on the banks of the Mississippi for his boat. "My

---

11. Lines 1–6 and 47–50 of "The Temple of God," a 60-line poem published in *Times and Seasons,* August 1, 1841. See *Complete Poetry,* 169–71.

12. Snow, "Sketch," in Beecher, *Personal Writings,* 18.

13. Snow's manuscript of "Retirement" may be seen on the facing page. Composed between November 10 and 30, 1842, it was not published during Snow's lifetime. See *Complete Poetry,* 227–28.

*"Retirement" (unpublished), written by Eliza in her journal
in November 1842, describes the blessings of solitude.*

heart overflowed with gratitude when, after the landing of the boat, I heard Prest. Hiram Smith say to me 'your brother has actually arrived.' It is a time of mutual rejoicing which I never shall forget."[14]

Nevertheless, the Illinois years were also a time of separation from some of her

---

14. Snow, Diary, April 12, 1843, in Beecher, *Personal Writings*, 74.

Emma Smith.

family members, both geographically and philosophically. Although her parents had been baptized in Ohio and followed the Saints to Missouri and then to Illinois, they subsequently distanced themselves from the Church under the stresses of persecution, age, and illness. In 1842, along with two of Eliza's younger brothers, they moved to Walnut Grove, Illinois, some ninety miles northeast of Nauvoo. To Eliza's great sorrow, her father died there in 1845, and her mother in 1846.

But as old family ties faded, new ones emerged to take their place. On June 29, 1842, Eliza R. Snow was sealed as a plural wife to Joseph Smith "for time and eternity, in accordance with the *Celestial Law of Marriage,* which God has revealed," she wrote.[15]

---

15. Snow, "Sketch," in Beecher, *Personal Writings,* 17.

Eliza stated that initially she found "very repugnant to my feelings"[16] the idea that Old Testament polygamy would be renewed in the latter days, but converted by her own reason, faith, and revelation, she accepted Joseph's invitation to become part of his extensive family. "As I increased in knowledge concerning the principle and design of Plural Marriage, I grew in love with it," she said.[17] She defended plural marriage for the rest of her life as a "precious, sacred principle."[18] Inevitably controversial, the multiple marriages of Joseph Smith and a small circle of confidential associates were not publicly acknowledged in Nauvoo. Even in her diary, which Eliza commenced on the day of her marriage, she did not make explicit mention of her new status but referred simply to "a day of much interest to my feelings."[19] Her poems for this period convey her deep admiration, concern, and affection for Joseph—she later described him as "the choice of my life and the crown of my heart"[20]—while simultaneously implying her frustration in having to keep her marriage secret.

Much speculation has swirled around the question of Eliza's relationship with Emma Smith. Given the fact that Eliza lived in the Smith household in Kirtland and Nauvoo and that she worked closely with Emma in the Female Relief Society of Nauvoo, there is every reason to suppose that the women were good friends. Indeed, Eliza later recalled that she "once dearly loved 'Sister Emma.'"[21] Eliza knew Emma to be a generous and kind woman, and she grieved for Emma's sorrows. In June 1841, Joseph Smith was arrested on unsubstantiated charges of treason dating back to Missouri. Here are some lines from the poem Eliza wrote on that occasion as she considered Emma's feelings:

---

16. Snow, "Sketch," in Beecher, *Personal Writings*, 16.
17. Snow, "Sketch," in Beecher, *Personal Writings*, 17.
18. Snow, "Sketch," in Beecher, *Personal Writings*, 17.
19. Snow, Diary, June 29, 1842, in Beecher, *Personal Writings*, 52.
20. "Past and Present," *Woman's Exponent* 15 (August 1886): 37.
21. Eliza R. Snow to Editors, *Deseret News*, October 17, 1879, in "Joseph the Seer's Plural Marriages. His Wife Emma's Consent Thereto," *Deseret News*, October 18, 1879, 2, reprinted in *Woman's Exponent* 8 (November 1, 1879): 84.

I saw her in the throng, that met to pray
For her companion—torn from her away,
And from the church; thro' the device of those,
Who in Missouri, vow'd to be our foes!
I gazed a moment, then I turn'd aside,
The agitation of my soul to hide;
And asked the Lord, to send a quick relief
To her, who ever wept o'er others' grief—
To her, whose presence heav'nly lustre shed—
Who cloth'd the naked, and the hungry fed.[22]

Clearly, there may well have been some conflict between Emma and Eliza over plural marriage. After Emma learned of the principle of plural marriage, she vacillated in her feelings, at times seeming to support the principle but at other times speaking against it. On February 11, 1843, after Eliza had been living in the Smith home about six months, Eliza made an abrupt note in her journal: "Took board and had my lodging removed to the residence of br. J. Holmes."[23] The circumstances that precipitated this move are unclear. Perhaps Emma asked Eliza to leave, but crowded circumstances in the household were more likely the cause of her departure. The day Eliza left, the Smiths were "changing the furniture in the house to receive mother Smith in the family."[24] Exactly why Eliza lived some thirty miles south of Nauvoo near Lima, Illinois, between July 1843 and April 1844, is another mystery. But after her return to Nauvoo, she reached out to Emma in a poem commemorating the

---

22. The poem to Emma Smith was published in *Times and Seasons,* June 15, 1841, without a title but with this introductory sentence: "The following lines were written during the late arrest of Pres. Joseph Smith, which was instigated through the untiring malice of Missouri persecution; and are respectfully inscribed to Mrs. Emma Smith." These are the first 10 lines of a 38-line poem. See *Complete Poetry,* 163–64.

23. Snow, "Sketch," in Beecher, *Personal Writings,* 64.

24. Joseph Smith Journal, as recorded by his clerk Willard Richards, February 11, 1843, in Hedges, Smith, and Anderson, eds., *Journals,* 2:262.

birth of David Hyrum Smith, Joseph and Emma's last child, born five months after Joseph was assassinated. The poem concludes with these lines addressed to infant David Hyrum:

> *Thou may'st draw from love and kindness*
> *All a mother can bestow;*
> *But alas! on earth, a father*
> *Thou art destin'd not to know!*[25]

While Latter-day Saints had found a place of refuge in Illinois, discord gradually eroded the peace. As early as June 1842, Eliza's poems began to reflect a changing atmosphere in Nauvoo. Tensions were mounting, and poem after poem revealed her worry over the new strains that beset Joseph Smith and his followers. Formerly faithful insiders betrayed the Prophet, and anti-Mormon outsiders became fiercer in their opposition as the population and political power of the Saints in Nauvoo increased. Although much of Eliza's Nauvoo poetry previously had appeared in *The Whig*, a non-Mormon newspaper published in neighboring Quincy, she now began to publish almost exclusively in *The Wasp* and *Times and Seasons*, Latter-day Saint publications printed in Nauvoo.

During this time, Joseph Smith was repeatedly arrested on charges of various kinds, and he often had to go into hiding to escape threats to his freedom and even to his life. Several of Eliza's poems during this difficult time expressed her anxiety for Joseph's safety and well-being. One of them, titled "Invocation," is a prayer for the protection of Joseph and his people:

> *O God! thou God that rules on high,*
> *Bow down thy ear to me;*
> *Listen, O listen to my cry—*
> *Hear thou, my fervent plea.*

---

25. The original poem on the birth of David Hyrum Smith is 32 lines long. Composed on November 24, 1844, it was published in *Times and Seasons*, December 1, 1844. See *Complete Poetry*, 302–3.

Rebuke the heartless, wicked clan
That fain would do us harm;
Protect us from the power of man,
By thy Almighty arm.

O hide him in thy secret fold
When on his path they tread;
Safe as Elijah who of old
Was by the ravens fed.[26]

During these trying months, the Saints celebrated a joyous moment that was memorialized by Eliza in a ballad titled "The Kidnapping of General Joseph Smith." From June 23 to June 30, 1843, Joseph was in the custody of a Missouri sheriff, Joseph H. Reynolds, and an Illinois constable, Harmon T. Wilson, who were intent on transporting him to Missouri to stand trial under an indictment for treason against that state. They had forced Joseph into a wagon at gunpoint with no writ of habeas corpus. Joseph was finally able to obtain a writ of habeas corpus for himself and a writ against Reynolds and Wilson for unlawful proceedings. The writs had to be tried in the nearest tribunal, which, ironically, turned out to be the municipal court in Nauvoo. Jubilant crowds greeted Joseph's return to Nauvoo. Joseph took the two officials home to dinner, and, as he explained, "set them at the head of my table, and placed before them the best which my house afforded."[27]

The case against Joseph Smith was ultimately dismissed. In the poem that follows, Eliza captured the suspense of the "kidnapping" and the elation of the Nauvoo citizens upon Joseph's return.[28]

---

26. Lines 1–8 and 21–24 of "Invocation," a 28-line poem published in *Times and Seasons,* September 1, 1842. Snow also included this poem in *Poems* (1856) under the title "Supplication." See *Complete Poetry,* 208–9.

27. Smith, *History of the Church,* 5:467.

28. The entire text of the poem is given here. Published in *Nauvoo Neighbor,* July 26, 1843, it was reprinted in *Times and Seasons* 4 (August 1, 1843): 288, and in Snow's *Poems* (1856), 127–29. See *Complete Poetry,* 244–46.

The Kidnapping of General Joseph Smith

Like bloodhounds fiercely prowling,
With pistols ready drawn—
With oaths like tempests howling,
Those kidnappers came on.

He bared his breast before them,
But as they hurried near,
A fearfulness came o'er them—
It was the coward's fear.

Well might their dark souls wither
When he their courage dared—
Their pity fled, O whither?
When he his bosom bared!

"Death has to me no terrors,"
He said, "I hate a life
So subject to the horrors
Of your ungodly strife."

"What means your savage conduct?
Have you a lawful writ?
To any LEGAL process
I cheerfully submit."

"Here" said these lawless ruffians,
"Is our authority;"
And drew their pistols nearer
In rude ferocity.

With more than savage wildness—
Like hungry beasts of prey;
They bore, in all his mildness,
The man of God away.

With brutish haste they tore him
From her he loves so well,
And far away they bore him
With scarce the word "farewell!"

Their hearts are seats where blindness
O'er foul corruption reigns—
The milk of human kindness,
Flows not within their veins.

Their conduct was unworthy
The meanest race of men;
'Twould better fit the tiger
Emerging from its den!

Missouri! O, Missouri!
You thus prolong your shame
By sending such as Reynolds
Abroad to bear your name.

Could Jackson County furnish
No tamer shrub than he?
Must legal office burnish
Such wild barbarity?

Go search the rudest forests,
The panther and the bear
As well would grace your suff'rage—
As well deserve a share.

Then might the heartless Wilson,
Thy shame, O Illinois!
Become confed'rate with them
And teach them to destroy.

So much ferocious nature　　　　　*But hear it, O Missouri!*
Should join the brutish clan,　　　*Once more "the prophet's free"—*
And not disgrace the features　　　*Your ill-directed fury*
That claim to be a man.　　　　　*Brings forth a "jubilee."*

In her diary, she described this unforgettable scene: "The affectionate manner in which he introduced his family to those worse than savage officers, and the very hospitable treatment they received, was a lesson that should have made an impression on every heart."[29]

The hostility between the Saints and their foes culminated in tragedy. On June 27, 1844, the Prophet was murdered. Many of the enemies of the Saints assumed that his death would mean the end of Mormonism, but Eliza's voice was among those urging the now leaderless Saints to remain united as a strong and faithful people. Within days of the martyrdom, she expressed her grief and outrage in a formal but impassioned lament for Joseph Smith and his brother Hyrum. Here is an excerpt from the eighty-four-line poem:

> *Great men have fall'n and mighty men have died—*
> *Nations have mourn'd their fav'rites and their pride;*
> *But TWO, so wise, so virtuous, great and good,*
> *Before on earth, at once, have never stood*
> *Since the creation—men whom God ordain'd*
> *To publish truth where error long had reigned;*
> *Of whom the world, itself unworthy prov'd:*
> *It KNEW THEM NOT; but men with hatred mov'd*
> *And with infernal spirits have combin'd*
> *Against the best, the noblest of mankind!*
> *We mourn thy Prophet, from whose lips have flow'd*
> *The words of life, thy spirit has bestow'd—*

---

29. Snow, Diary, June 30, 1842, in Beecher, *Personal Writings*, 78.

A depth of thought, no human art could reach

From time to time, roll'd in sublimest speech,

From the celestial fountain, through his mind,

To purify and elevate mankind:

One in their life, and one in death—they prov'd

How strong their friendship—how they truly lov'd:

True to their mission, until death, they stood,

Then seal'd their testimony with their blood.[30]

Years later Eliza maintained restraint in describing her private grief at "the awful trajedy of the 27th of June 1844." She remembered "the noble lifeless forms of those brothers, Joseph and Hyrum Smith, lying side by side," and noted: "What it was for loving wives and children, the loyal heart may <u>feel</u>, but let <u>language keep silence</u>!"[31]

In the course of the Nauvoo years, Eliza had separated herself from her parents' household, geographically and religiously, and the death of Joseph left her once again without the protection and security of family ties. She was married to Brigham Young for time in October 1844, but it would be more than two years before this second marriage could offer the security of a true family and home. As she faced the move to the West, she was surrounded by like-minded Saints who respected her as a poet and as a leader of the now disbanded Female Relief Society of Nauvoo.[32] Though Joseph Smith and then Brigham Young had arranged for her to live in the Nauvoo home of Stephen and Hannah Markham, Eliza nevertheless was ultimately alone. As the Saints

---

30. Lines 41–50, 59–64, and 71–74 of an 84-line poem first published in *Times and Seasons* July 1, 1844, four days after the assassination. See *Complete Poetry*, 295–99.

31. Snow, "Sketch," in Beecher, *Personal Writings*, 17.

32. The last recorded meeting of the Female Relief Society of Nauvoo was held March 16, 1844. Brigham Young later supported reorganization of ward Relief Societies in Utah Territory. See Derr, Cannon, and Beecher, *Women of Covenant*, 119–26.

OPPOSITE: *This single-page rendering of Eliza's poem on the assassination of Joseph and Hyrum Smith was printed after it appeared in* Times and Seasons *July 1, 1844, in Nauvoo. The original rendering measured 9.8 by 7.5 inches and was designed as a memorial keepsake of the tragic event.*

LINES

ON THE

ASSASSINATION OF GENERALS JOSEPH SMITH & HYRUM SMITH,

First Presidents of the Church of Latter-Day Saints,

WHO WERE

MASSACRED BY A MOB IN CARTHAGE, HANCOCK COUNTY, ILLINOIS,

ON THE TWENTY-SEVENTH JUNE, 1844.

BY MISS ELIZA R. SNOW.

And when he had opened the fifth seal, I saw under the altar, the souls of them that were slain for the word of God, and for the testimony which they held.

And they cried with a loud voice, saying, How long, O Lord, holy and true, dost thou not judge and avenge our blood on them that dwell on the earth?

And white robes were given unto every one of them; and it was said unto them, that they should rest yet for a little season, until their fellow-servants also, and their brethren, that should be killed as they were, should be fulfilled.—Rev. vi. 9, 10, 11.

Ye heavens attend! Let all the earth give ear!
Let Gods and seraphs, men and angels hear—
The worlds on high—the universe shall know
What awful scenes are acted here below!
Had nature's self a heart, her heart would bleed;
For never, since the Son of God was slain,
Has blood so noble, flowed from human vein
As that which now on God for vengeance calls
From "freedom's ground"—from Carthage's prison walls.

Oh, Illinois! thy soil has drank the blood
Of Prophets martyr'd for the truth of God.
Once-lov'd America! what can atone
For the pure blood of innocence, thou'st sown?
Were all thy streams in teary torrents shed
To mourn the fate of those illustrious dead:
How vain the tribute, for the noblest worth
That grac'd thy surface, O degraded Earth!

Oh, wretched murderers! fierce for human blood!
You've slain the prophets of the living God,
Who've borne oppression from their early youth,
To plant on earth the principles of truth.

Shades of our patriotic fathers! Can it be,
Beneath your blood-stain'd flag of liberty,
The firm supporters of our country's cause
Are butcher'd, while submissive to her laws?
Yes, blameless men, defam'd by hellish lies,
Have thus been offer'd as a sacrifice
T' appease the ragings of a brutish clan,
That has defied the laws of God and man!

'Twas not for crime or guilt of theirs they fell—
Against the laws they never did rebel.
True to their country, yet her plighted faith
Has prov'd an instrument of cruel death!

Where are thy far-fam'd laws—Columbia? where
Thy boasted freedom?—thy protecting care?
Is this a land of rights? Stern facts shall say,
If legal justice here maintains its sway,
The' official powers of State are sheer pretence
When they're exerted in the Saints' defence.

Great men have fallen, and mighty men have died—
Nations have mourn'd their favourites and their pride;
But TWO, so wise, so virtuous, great and good,
Before, on earth, at once have never stood

Since the creation—men whom God ordain'd
To publish truth where error long had reign'd:
Of whom the world itself unworthy proved:
It KNEW THEM NOT; but men with hatred moved
And with infernal spirits have combin'd
Against the best, the noblest of mankind!

Oh, persecution! shall thy purple hand
Spread utter destruction through the land?
Shall freedom's banner be no more unfurl'd?
Has peace, indeed, been taken from the world?

Thou God of Jacob, in this trying hour
Help us to trust in thy almighty power;
Support thy Saints beneath this awful stroke—
Make bare thine arm to break oppression's yoke.
We mourn thy Prophet, from whose lips have flow'd
The words of life thy Spirit has bestow'd—
A depth of thought no human art could reach,
From time to time, roll'd in sublimest speech
From the celestial fountain through his mind,
To purify and elevate mankind:
The rich intelligence by him brought forth
Is like the sunbeam spreading o'er the earth.

Now Zion mourns—she mourns an earthly head:
The Prophet and the Patriarch are dead!
The blackest deed that men or devils know
Since Calvary's scene, has laid the brothers low!
One in their life, and one in death—they prov'd
How strong their friendship—how they truly lov'd:
True to their mission, until death they stood,
Then seal'd their testimony with their blood.
All hearts with sorrow bleed, and every eye
Is bath'd in tears—each bosom heaves a sigh—
Heart-broken widows' agonizing groans
Are mingled with the helpless orphans' moans!

Ye Saints! be still, and know that God is just—
With steadfast purpose in his promise trust:
Girded with sackcloth, own his mighty hand,
And wait his judgments on this guilty land!
The noble martyrs now have gone to move
The cause of Zion in the courts above.

Nauvoo, July 1st, 1844.

J. HEAP,   PRINTER.

prepared to leave Nauvoo, the daunting prospect of a long trek to a new refuge, under a new leader, and without close associates, must have required her to search within herself for even greater resources of courage and faith

In October 1845, following the death of her father, Oliver Snow, and in the midst of personal loneliness and uncertainty, Eliza wrote the last of her nearly one hundred Nauvoo poems. "O My Father" is her most beloved poem, one that has touched millions of hearts. For all Saints, it expresses a personal connectedness to God, from pre-mortal past, to earthly present, to eternal future. Most memorably, perhaps, it articulates the doctrine of a Mother in Heaven. For Eliza, it also expressed a displaced person's longing for a home; note such words as "dwellest," "habitation," "stranger," and "wandered." The poem bears eloquent testimony of the one home that she knew would one day be hers—her celestial home with her heavenly parents.

O My Father

O my Father, thou that dwellest
In the high and glorious place;
When shall I regain thy presence,
And again behold thy face?
In thy holy habitation
Did my spirit once reside?
In my first primeval childhood
Was I nurtur'd near thy side?

For a wise and glorious purpose
Thou hast plac'd me here on earth,
And withheld the recollection
Of my former friends and birth:
Yet oft times a secret something
Whispered you're a stranger here;
And I felt that I had wandered
From a more exalted sphere.

I had learn'd to call thee father
Through thy spirit from on high;
But until the key of knowledge
Was restor'd, I knew not why.
In the heav'ns are parents single?
No, the thought makes reason stare;
Truth is reason—truth eternal
Tells me I've a mother there.

When I leave this frail existence—
When I lay this mortal by,
Father, mother, may I meet you
In your royal court on high?
Then, at length, when I've completed
All you sent me forth to do,
With your mutual approbation
Let me come and dwell with you.[33]

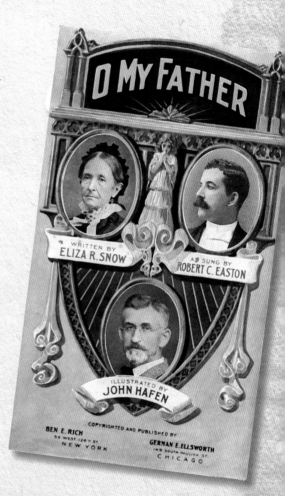

The conviction and faith that had grown within Eliza while living in her beloved "City of Joseph" continued to sustain her through the next four decades of what she termed her "variegated life."[34]

---

33. This poem first appeared in *Times and Seasons,* December 15, 1845, and has been reprinted many times since, both as a poem and as a hymn text. See *Complete Poetry,* 312–14; *Hymns,* no. 292.

34. Snow, "Sketch," in Beecher, *Personal Writings,* 6.

ABOVE: *Booklet with text and music from Eliza's hymn and illustrations by John Hafen. Published in 1909 by Ben E. Rich and German Ellsworth.*

Winter Quarters, *by C. C. A. Christensen. Eliza lived for ten months in Winter Quarters, a settlement along the Missouri River near present-day Council Bluffs, Nebraska. In these difficult circumstances, she wrote many poems of consolation and encouragement.*

Chapter Four

IN PURSUIT OF A LAND OF PEACE

1846–1847

On February 12, 1846, Eliza R. Snow packed her scant personal belongings and left Nauvoo, Illinois. "Cross'd the Mississippi and join'd the Camp,"[1] she wrote the next day in a small, tan leather diary, one of two she kept while on the trail.

Eliza's journey from Nauvoo to the valley of the Great Salt Lake lasted twenty-one months, from February 1846 to October 1847. In company with other Latter-day Saints, she traveled across Iowa Territory, wintered along the Missouri River, and then crossed unorganized territory to the Great Salt Lake Valley, a corner of the Mexican province then known as Upper California. She left behind in Illinois her sister Amanda, brothers Lucius and Samuel, her mother, and the grave of her father. Two other siblings, Leonora and Lorenzo, trekked west with the Saints but in a different wagon company.

Nauvoo had given the Saints a place of refuge from the persecutions of Missouri, the chance to establish homes and farms, and the time to complete a temple and there participate in holy ordinances. At its peak, the city had been home to more than eleven thousand people. But even after the murder of the Prophet Joseph on June 27, 1844, political and religious conflicts between the Saints and their neighbors

---

1. Snow, Diary, in Beecher, *Personal Writings,* 113.

*Final Farewell, by Glen Hopkinson. "Cross'd the Mississippi and join'd the Camp,"
Eliza wrote matter-of-factly in her diary on February 13, 1846.*

continued. Because of the threat of continued violence, the citizens of Nauvoo were forced to evacuate the city. Beginning in early February 1846, the Quorum of the Twelve Apostles, under the leadership of Brigham Young, instructed the Saints to prepare to leave. Over the next three weeks they assembled on the Iowa side of the Mississippi River in a place called Sugar Creek. The Mormons' historic westward trek had begun.

Eliza's travel arrangements for her departure from Nauvoo were made for her by Brigham Young, to whom she had been married for time as a plural wife on October 3, 1844. She did not take his surname, but he became her provider and protector, and she became a member of his family and household. She seems to have noted in her diary every conversation with "Brigham," "Prest. B. Y." or "B" as they moved along the trail in close proximity. She sustained Brigham Young as the head of the Church, the

the inheritor of Joseph Smith's prophetic mantle, and she defended his station with a fierce loyalty which she expressed in many of her poems.

Although the Saints did not know where they would eventually settle in the West, Eliza quickly caught the vision of a refuge where "the mountains of Israel in majesty rise."[2] As the Saints faced their daunting journey to the West, she wrote courageous, energetic poems describing the promise of a peaceful and glorious future in their new home. Perhaps at no other time did her verse serve a more vital purpose for the Saints than in the three "journeying songs" she wrote soon after leaving Nauvoo.[3] In a temporary camp in Sugar Creek, Iowa, in temperatures so low that the Saints had walked across the frozen Mississippi, she quickly penned lines for them to sing, lines that would help the new exiles view their mission in the loftiest and most optimistic terms.

One of these remarkable songs, written the day of the Saints' departure from Sugar Creek, not only portrays camp life in unusual and vivid detail but repaints the whole scene. The hardships of the present time, under her pen, symbolize the strength and destiny of the Lord's chosen people—Israel. It had been a time of bitter cold in Sugar Creek, with melting snow dripping through inadequate tents and with some of

---

2. Line 16 of the 32-line "Song for the Camp of Israel." See *Complete Poetry,* 323–24.

3. The three songs titled in Snow's diary "A Song for the Pioneers," "Song for the Pioneers. No. 2. Camp of Israel," and "Song for the Pioneers of the Camp of Israel, No. 3 Let Us Go," are poems 154, 155, and 156 in *Complete Poetry,* 319–26.

ABOVE: *Photograph of Eliza R. Snow, 1866, by Savage & Ottinger.*

the Saints suffering sickness and even death. As the poem indicates, they still feared for their safety. Yet Eliza saw these ragged tents and shivering Saints as the Camp of Israel, the "mighty host of Jacob," the people chosen to carry out God's purposes in the latter days. Her refrain "all is well," echoing the watchman's cry, predated by a few months William Clayton's use of those words in the pioneer anthem now titled "Come, Come, Ye Saints," which was written April 15, 1846.[4] She copied this "Song for the Pioneers" into her trail diary, retitling it "Song for the Camp of Israel" when she published it a decade later. Though clearly this, like many of Eliza's poems, was meant to be sung, we do not know which melody she had in mind. Several hymn tunes sung today by Latter-day Saints could be matched with these words, including "O Thou Rock of Our Salvation" and "They, the Builders of the Nation."[5]

Song for the Camp of Israel

Lo! a mighty host of Jacob
  Tented on the western shore
Of the noble Mississippi,
  Which they had been crossing o'er;
At the last day's dawn of winter,
  Bound with frost and wrapt in snow:
Hark! the sound is onward, onward!
  Camp of Israel! rise and go.

All at once is life and motion,
  Trunks and beds, and baggage fly;
Oxen yok'd and horses harness'd,—
  Tents roll'd up, are passing by;
Soon the carriage-wheels are rolling
  Onward to a woodland dell,

---

4. *Hymns* (1985), no. 30.
5. *Hymns* (1985), nos. 258 and 36, respectively.

Where, at sunset, all are quarter'd:
Camp of Israel! all is well.

Thickly round the tents are cluster'd
Neighbouring smokes, together blend;
Supper serv'd, the hymns are chanted,
And the evening prayers ascend.
Last of all the guards are station'd:
Heavens! must guards be serving here;
Who would harm the houseless exiles?
Camp of Israel! never fear.

Where is freedom? Where is justice?
Both have from this nation fled;
And the blood of martyr'd prophets
Must be answer'd on its head!
Therefore, to your tents, O Jacob!
Like our father Abram dwell;
God will execute his purpose:
Camp of Israel! all is well.[6]

Eliza traveled across Iowa Territory with the family of Hannah and Stephen Markham, friends of Joseph Smith with whom she had lived during her last two years in Nauvoo. With considerable good humor, she writes of conditions on the trek: "My dormitory, sitting-room, writing office, and frequently dining-room, was the buggy in which Mrs. Markham, her little son David, and I rode. With the best I could do for myself, I frosted my feet which occasioned me considerable inconvenience for several weeks. . . . [Yet] we were thankful to be so well off—fleeing from persecution, we were

---

6. This poem is presented here in its entirety. Written on March 1, 1846, it was published in *Millennial Star*, July 1, 1848. See *Complete Poetry*, 321–22.

in pursuit of a land of peace."[7] She was particularly impressed by the strength of the women of the company, many of whom "walked all day, rain or shine," rather than ride in the relative luxury of a wagon, and who "at night prepared supper for their families, with no sheltering tents. . . . Frequently with intense sympathy and admiration I watched the mother when, forgetful of her own fatigue and destitution, she took unwearied pains to fix up in the most palatable form the allotted portion (most of the time we were rationed) of food, and as she dealt it out, was cheering the hearts of her children, while, as I truly believed, her own was lifted to God in fervent prayer that their lives might be preserved."[8]

The ill-provisioned Saints made their way along rough trails and often through deep mud. By May, Eliza had arrived at the way station known as Mount Pisgah, where the Saints planted gardens to be harvested by those who followed. Here her brother Lorenzo fell severely ill. "I feel great reason for thankfulness that the Lord has given me strength to administer to L.,"[9] she wrote in her diary on June 11. Two weeks later she penned a prayer: "O Lord my God I pray for health that I may be useful."[10] The 265-mile journey across Iowa Territory, which the Saints anticipated would take three or four weeks, took nearly sixteen. But Eliza continued to make the best of every situation. "It is a growling, grumbling, devilish, sickly time with us now—I hope never to see another week like the past one. . . . Have been a little at loss how to do, but conclude to see the game thro', & enjoy the scenery."[11]

Notes about the weather and the landscape dot Eliza's diary: "The month commences with a volley of natures tears quite cold,"[12] "bluffs rudely scallop'd with shrubbery presented a scene that might well be call'd wildly beautiful."[13] At one point, when

---

7. Snow, "Sketch," in Beecher, *Personal Writings,* 19–20.

8. Snow, "Sketch," in Beecher, *Personal Writings,* 21.

9. Snow, Diary, June 11, 1846, in Beecher, *Personal Writings,* 136.

10. Snow, Diary, June 24, 1846, in Beecher, *Personal Writings,* 137.

11. Snow, Diary, August 10 [9], 1846, in Beecher, *Personal Writings,* 139.

12. Snow, Diary, June 1, 1846, in Beecher, *Personal Writings,* 135.

13. Snow, Diary, August 28 [27], 1846, in Beecher, *Personal Writings,* 142.

Sister Markham fell ill, the task of driving the ox team fell to Eliza. "Had it been a horse team," she wrote, "I should have been amply qualified, but driving oxen was entirely new business. However, I took the whip, and very soon learned to *haw* and *jee,* and acquitted myself very well in driving most of the way to 'Winter Quarters.'"[14]

After crossing Iowa, the Saints stopped for the winter in encampments along the Missouri River. The largest of their temporary settlements, called Winter Quarters, was in the unorganized territory that became Nebraska. Eliza arrived there with the Markhams in early August. "I go to my trade—make pr. pants for David [the Markham's youngest son],"[15] she wrote on August 29. Then, two days later, she fell seriously ill "from exposure and hardship."[16] For forty days she lay sick with fever in her wagon, where her bed "was exposed to heavy rains, and, at times, unavoidably wet from head to foot[.] I realized that I was near the gate of death; but in this suffering and exposed condition, I did not feel that God had forsaken me—my trust was in Him, and His power preserved me. While passing through this trying scene, I not only realized the goodness of God, but experienced many kindnesses from my sisters, whose names are not only written in my Journal, but also are engraven on my heart."[17] Her poems pay tribute to the kindness of Vilate Kimball, Mary Ann Young, Leonora Taylor, Margarett Peirce Whitesides, and many other women with whom she formed deep and warm friendships that would sustain her for the rest of her life.

Sickness and death were ever present on the trail and in the camps. Eliza wrote of seeing "the funeral train following to its *wilderness grave* a little child of br. Turley. It was a lonely sight—my feelings truly sympathize with those who are call'd to leave their dear relatives by the way."[18] Many of the poems Eliza wrote while on the trail memorialize individual Saints, both children and adults, who died during the trek; they bear such titles as "Lines on the death of three small children" and "On the death of

---

14. Snow, "Sketch," in Beecher, *Personal Writings,* 23.

15. Snow, Diary, August 29, 1846, in Beecher, *Personal Writings,* 143.

16. Snow, "Sketch" and Diary, mid-September 1846, in Beecher, *Personal Writings,* 23–24, 143.

17. Snow, "Sketch," in Beecher, *Personal Writings,* 23–24.

18. Snow, Diary, May 13, 1846, in Beecher, *Personal Writings,* 133.

Mary." One of those poems was a poem of comfort to Eliza Marie Partridge Lyman, with whom Eliza felt a sisterly tie because both women had previously been sealed to Joseph Smith as plural wives in Nauvoo. Following Joseph's death, Eliza Marie married Amasa Lyman, and their baby, Don Carlos, was born in a wagon on July 14, 1846, as the Saints crossed Iowa Territory. But the baby fared poorly from birth; he died on December 12, 1846. Two days later, Eliza Snow copied this poem into her diary, along with the prayer, "O Lord, comfort the heart of the mother in this sudden bereavement":

> *Belov'd Eliza, do not weep*
> *Your baby sleeps a quiet sleep;*
> *Altho' in dust its body lies*
> *Its spirit soars above the skies.*[19]

In December 1846, while at Winter Quarters, Eliza received word from Illinois that her mother had died. In her diary Eliza wrote that she felt in this news "a sweet consolation inasmuch as she is freed from the ills of the present life. . . . She sleeps in peace & her grave & father's, who died a year ago the 18th of last Oct., are side by side." Now without father or mother, Eliza wrote a poem honoring the memory of her parents. She drew the meter for this poem from a popular tune of the time, "The Indian Hunter," a plaintive ballad that evokes both longing and hope. Eliza first appropriated this ballad with a trail song beginning "Let us go—Let us go."

> *They are gone—they are gone to a kingdom of rest—*
> *They are gone—they are gone to the home of the blest*
> *Far away from the ills of this lower abode—*
> *They have gone to reside in a mansion of God.*[20]

---

19. Lines 1–4 of a 16-line poem. Snow, Diary, December 14, 1846, in Beecher, *Personal Writings,* 149. Snow copied this unpublished poem into her 1842–1882 journal, a separate volume that contains her Nauvoo diary entries and later letters and poems. The journal is in Church History Library, The Church of Jesus Christ of Latter-day Saints, Salt Lake City, Utah. See *Complete Poetry,* 331–32.

20. Verse 1 of a 3-verse poem unpublished in Snow's lifetime. Snow, Diary, December 22, 1846, in Beecher, *Personal Writings,* 150. See *Complete Poetry,* 332–33.

Eliza's journal contains this drawing for her friend Sarah Kimball.

Mingled with poems of loss that reflect the inevitable sorrows of the pioneer experience are many poems of faith, hope, joy, friendship, and community. The forward-looking energy of the trail poems, the happy, grateful sentiments expressed to other women, the encouragement and praise of missionaries and Church leaders, all speak of an optimism and resilience that are part of a remarkable picture of the journey to the Salt Lake Valley.

Ann Alice Geen (or Gheen) Kimball was one of many women with whom Eliza established a friendship on the trip westward. Ann's mother, Hester Geen, was among those who cared for Eliza when she was bedridden for much of September and October 1846, and Ann also was known for her kindness. Eliza wrote a poem of tribute and gratitude to Ann, whom she referred to as "Anna," using a poetic device known as an acrostic: the first letters of each line spell out "Miss Anna Geen":

Acrostic for Anna Geen

M=*ay the spirit of contentment,*
I=*n your bosom ever dwell;*
S=*uch as in the hour of trial*
S=*weetly whispers, "all is well."*

A=*s the blooming rose of summer*
N=*e'er withdraws its fragrant breath*
N=*ever may your love and friendship*
A=*nd your kindness cease till death.*

G=*reatness, goodness, light and wisdom,*
E=*ndless happiness and peace,*
E=*vermore adorn your pathway—*
N=*ever shall your blessings cease.*[21]

When Parley P. Pratt and John Taylor, both members of the Twelve, arrived in Winter Quarters in early April 1847, they reported their missionary successes in England. The excitement surrounding this missionary work was the likely motive for Eliza's first poem to the overseas Saints, which was published in the *Millennial Star* in Liverpool, an official Church periodical. At that time, converts were encouraged to leave their native countries to gather with fellow members of the Church in America.

Eliza offered encouragement to the new converts overseas and assured them of the love of their brothers and sisters on the American side of the Atlantic[22]:

---

21. The unpublished poem to Anna Geen is quoted here in its entirety. Snow, Diary, March 4, 1847, in Beecher, *Personal Writings,* 156. See *Complete Poetry,* 337–38.
22. Lines 1–8, 13–16, and 25–32 of a 32-line poem published in *Millennial Star,* December 15, 1847. See *Complete Poetry,* 351–52.

To the Saints in Great Britain

Ye Saints who dwell on Europe's shore,
Let not your hearts be faint:
Let each press on to things before,
And be indeed a Saint.

Although the present time may seem
O'erspread with clouds of gloom,
The light of faith will shed its gleam
Until deliv'rance come.

Your brethren, in America,
Are one in heart with you;

And they are toiling, night and day,
For Zion's welfare, too.

Then brethren haste, and gather up,
We shall rejoice to meet;
When we have drunk the bitter cup,
We'll share a heavenly treat.

And even now the Lord bestows
More—more than tongue can tell,
Of that which from His presence flows—
Yes, Brethren,—"all is well."

Music was an important inspiration and morale builder for the exiled Saints. "Many, yes many were the star and moonlight evenings," Eliza wrote, "when, as we circled around the blazing fire and sang our hymns of devotion and songs of praise to Him . . . united voices reverberated from hill to hill . . . echoing through the silent expanse, . . . while the glory of God seemed to rest on all around us."[23] In a poem titled "Song of the Desert," she described the pleasure of singing together:

Beneath the cloud-topp'd mountain,
Beside the craggy bluff,
Where every dint of nature
Is rude and wild enough;
Upon the verdant meadow,
Upon the sunburnt plain,
Upon the sandy hillock;
We waken music's strain.

---

23. Snow, "Sketch," in Beecher, *Personal Writings*, 28.

Cheer'd by the blaze of firelight,
When twilight shadows fall,
And when the darkness gathers
Around our spacious hall,
With all the warm emotion
To saintly bosoms given,
In strains of pure devotion
We praise the God of heaven.[24]

In April 1847, as the first company left Winter Quarters to travel the final six hundred miles west, Eliza wrote a song to encourage them. This "vanguard company," composed of 143 men, three women, and two children, would arrive in the valley of the Great Salt Lake in July. Eliza did not travel with this first company, but she wrote in her diary that "Prest. Y." had asked her to write a "journeying song" to lift the spirits of the vanguard and other pioneer Saints as they traveled west. The song she copied into her diary evidently became quite popular; multiple copies have come down to us, handwritten by Brigham Young's clerks and including the notation "Auld Lang Syne" as the tune. The chorus (stanza 2) is to be sung after each verse:

A Journeying Song for the Camp of Israel

The time of winter now is o'er—
  There's verdure on the plain;
We leave our shelt'ring roofs once more,
  And to our tents again.

  CHORUS.
Thou Camp of Israel! onward move—
  O Jacob! rise and sing.

24. Stanzas 1 and 4 of the 32-line poem "Song of the Desert." Snow, Diary, August 26, 1847, in Beecher, *Personal Writings*, 195–96. See *Complete Poetry*, 360–62.

Ye Saints! the world's salvation prove,
  All hail! to Zion's King.

We leave the mobbing Gentile race,
  Who thirst to shed our blood;
To rest in Jacob's hiding place
  Where Nephite temples stood.

We'll find the land the prophet saw
  In Vision, when he said;
"There, there will the celestial law
  Be given and obey'd."

We go where nations yet will come
  In ships, from climes abroad;
To seek protection, and a home,
  And worship Israel's God.

We'll build in peace and safety there,
  A city to the Lord:
And shout amid our toils to share
  A Latter-day's reward.[25]

Mary Ann Angell Young, like Eliza, remained behind in Winter Quarters while their husband, Brigham Young, traveled westward with the small vanguard pioneer company. Brigham and Mary Ann, married in Kirtland, Ohio, in 1834, were the parents of six children, but as plural marriage expanded the Young family, Mary Ann's "mothering extended to all of her husband's many children, who fondly called her

---

25. Lines 1–8, 25–28, and 45–56 of a poem recorded in Snow, Diary, March 18, 1847, with the note "transcrib'd the following which I had written some weeks ago by the request of Prest Y." In Beecher, *Personal Writings*, 160. See *Complete Poetry*, 344–46.

'Mother Young.'"[26] Since leaving Illinois, Eliza had drawn close to Brigham Young's other wives—"beloved sisters," she called them, "for whom my love seem'd to increase with every day's acquaintance."[27] The Young wives and other women, including several widows of Joseph Smith, formed a circle that met to strengthen one another and share such gifts of the Spirit as healing, prophecy, and speaking in tongues. "We enjoyed much of the Spirit of God, and many seasons of refreshing from His presence,"[28] Eliza remembered.

The shared exercise of the spiritual gifts of tongues, prophecy, and healing among Brigham Young's wives and other women at Winter Quarters provided spiritual renewal and refreshment for women who were exhausted from travel, sickness, privation, and the death of loved ones. In a poem addressed "To all the Ladies Who Reside in the 2d Mansion of Prest. B. Young," a playful reference to the small cabins in which her sister-wives lived in Winter Quarters, Eliza celebrated the gift of tongues as well as the love and sisterhood they shared[29]:

> *Beloved sisters all unite.*
> *In music's sweetest strains—*
> *'Twill prove a fountain of delight*
> *While love with you remains.*
>
> *Songs of the righteous, saith the Lord*
> *Are prayers unto me—*
> *Our spirits prove the rich reward*
> *Of sacred harmony.*
>
> *Let not a gift be buried low*
> *That with a proper care*
> *And cultivation will bestow*
> *Celestial pleasure there.*
>
> *What wisdom dictates for our good*
> *Should be our steady aim;*
> *And no excuse should e'er intrude*
> *Where <u>duty</u> holds a claim.*

---

26. Madsen, *In Their Own Words,* 140, quoting "LDS Women of the Past," *Woman's Exponent* 36 (May 1908): 66.

27. Snow, Diary, January 1, 1847, in Beecher, *Personal Writings,* 151.

28. Snow, "Sketch," in Beecher, *Personal Writings,* 24.

29. Verses 1–4 of an 8-verse unpublished poem, recorded in Snow's diary, January 26, 1847. See *Complete Poetry,* 334–36; underlining in original.

Winter Quarters, *by Greg Olsen.*

The frequent gatherings of women at Winter Quarters, described by Eliza in her diary as "a glorious time" and "a treat of the spirit,"[30] bound her to her new family, her sister-wives. On June 12, 1847, when she left Winter Quarters to begin the journey to Salt Lake Valley, she wrote, "Bade farewell to many who seem dearer to me than life."[31]

Traveling with Captain Jedediah M. Grant's company, Eliza was part of the third of four companies of one hundred people each who left Winter Quarters in June 1847. She traveled in the wagon of the Peirce family, which included Robert and Mary Harvey Peirce and their twenty-four-year-old daughter Margarett, who was another of Brigham Young's wives. The Peirce family and Eliza remained the closest of friends from that time on.

Eliza recorded in her diary that on September 8, 1847, her company met Brigham Young, Heber C. Kimball, and others who were traveling eastward to Winter Quarters to shepherd their families and other Saints to the valley of the Great Salt Lake, the Saints' newly designated gathering place. It was a significant reunion for Eliza and Brigham who knew that a full year would pass before they saw each other again. Eliza recorded their conversation in her diary: "Before the P[eirce]s left B[righam] came to the carriage blest us—I ask'd who was to be my counsellor for the year to come—he said E. R. S. I said 'she is not capable'—he said 'I have appointed her president'—said

---

30. Snow, Diary, June 6 and June 18, 1847, in Beecher, *Personal Writings,* 176, 179.
31. Snow, Diary, June 12, 1847, in Beecher, *Personal Writings,* 177.

he had conversation with br. P[eirce] about provision—that he will furnish me & all will be right."[32] Eliza looked to Brigham as provider and protector, and he both arranged for her support and expressed confidence in her ability to act independently. She proved worthy of his trust. While writing, sewing, ironing, cooking, picking currants, and even submitting her diary to assist "in making up the history of the Camp from W. Quarters," Eliza traveled to the Great Salt Lake Valley and there took charge of her life, despite her continued ill health.[33]

The day after the two companies met, they assembled in the evening to hear preaching from Church leaders and to sing, wrote Eliza, "a song . . . I had written."[34] Following are stanzas from that song, written to be sung to a tune the pioneers knew as "Yes, My Native Land, I Love Thee." The "hiding place" referred to in the first verse is the Great Salt Lake Valley, where Eliza will bid the travelers "welcome home" after they circled back to Winter Quarters and then returned once more with their families to the Saints' new gathering place.

Hail to the Twelve and Pioneers

Hail ye mighty men of Israel,
Who the hiding place have found;
The eternal God has blest you,
You have stood on holy ground.

CHORUS.
Praise the Lord, we're glad to meet you,
Welcome, welcome, on the way;
Yes, O yes, with songs we greet you,
Pioneers of Latter Day.

---

32. Snow, Diary, September 10, 1847, in Beecher, *Personal Writings*, 199.
33. Snow, Diary, January 1, 1848, in Beecher, *Personal Writings*, 216.
34. Snow, Diary, September 10, 1847, in Beecher, *Personal Writings*, 199.

OPPOSITE: *The plaid blanket was woven by Eliza in her youth and taken by her to the West. The spoon, with monogram ERS, was also Eliza's. The portrait of Brigham Young is by William Major, painted about 1850.*

> *Holy, free, and unpolluted,*
> *Will that land for us remain,*
> *While the sacred laws of justice*
> *Will the Saints of God maintain.*
>
> *Go, return, to winter quarters;*
> *Go in peace and safety too;*
> *There the purest hearts are beating,*
> *Warm with hopes of seeing you.*
>
> *We will onward to the valley,*
> *Speed your way, make haste and come,*
> *That ere long with joy and gladness*
> *We may bid you welcome home.*[35]

The longed-for day finally arrived. Eliza's company reached the Great Salt Lake Valley on October 2, 1847. As she described it in her diary, "About 4 we come in view of the Valley looking like a broad rich river bottom."[36] In her autobiographical sketch, she continued her description of life in the Saints' new home: "Our first winter in the mountains was delightful—the ground froze very little [and] the temperature truly seemed to have been particularly ordered to meet our very peculiar circumstances."[37] Brigham Young had made arrangements for her to live with a sister-wife, Clarissa (often called Clara) Decker Young. The log cabin was small, and the roof inadequate to keep out the rain. But she had arrived in "the Valley," sharing the joy of her fellow Saints in their promised refuge.

On her third day in the Great Salt Lake Valley, Eliza wrote eleven letters to "send to W. Q. [Winter Quarters]." Among them she included a poem dedicated "to sis. Whitney, Kimball, Sarah A. & Helen," who were Elizabeth Ann Smith Whitney, Vilate

---

35. Lines 1–8 and 13–24 of a 24-line poem. See *Complete Poetry*, 363–64.
36. Snow, Diary, October 2, 1847, in Beecher, *Personal Writings*, 204.
37. Snow, "Sketch," in Beecher, *Personal Writings*, 29.

Murray Kimball, and their daughters Sarah Ann Whitney Kimball and Helen Mar Kimball Whitney, friends whom she had left behind in Winter Quarters. On the same day she penned lines for Mary Ann Angell Young. She missed the women's friendship, and she wanted them to share in the joy of the Saints' new home. She later combined the two poems and published them under the title "Come to the Valley":

All is well, is well in Zion—
Zion is the pure in heart:
Come along, you holy women,
And your blessings here impart.

May rich streams of consolation
Ever to your bosoms flow,
And the bitterness of sorrow
Be no more your lots to know.

I anticipate the period
When you to the Valley come:
Haste and leave your Winter Quarters—
Here you'll find a better home.[38]

38. Lines 9–16, 21–24. Snow, Diary, October 5, 1847, in Beecher, *Personal Writings,* 204–5. Composed on October 5, 1847, the poems were combined and published in Snow's *Poems* (1856). See *Complete Poetry,* 366–67.

State Street Panorama, *by Al Rounds. Shown in this artist's re-creation of a scene in old Salt Lake City in the late 1800s are the Lion House, where Eliza took up residence in 1856; the Beehive House; and the Eagle Gate monument, built in 1859 to mark the entrance to Brigham Young's property.*

Chapter Five

WHERE THE SPIRIT IS FREE

1847–1865

W e had a refreshing time,"[1] Eliza wrote in her diary on Sunday, October 31, 1847. She had met that day with dear friends—Patty Sessions, Abigail Leonard, Lucina Chase, Clarissa Decker Young, and others who were starting life anew in the valley of the Great Salt Lake. Eliza had entered the valley on October 2, 1847, little more than two months after the historic arrival of the Saints' "vanguard company" on July 24. She regularly recorded in her diary the simple pleasures and common privations of her new beginning in the wilderness the Saints now called home. She described the October weather as "quite warm" and then a week later "too cold for me to sit out at meeting."[2] On November 2, snow fell. Food was scarce enough that she noted the bits and pieces she received: two quarts of meal and a little flour, two quarts of beans, four sea biscuits, a quart of dried apples, a piece of beef. When she made a cap for a friend, she was paid in soap: "1 lb. & 15 oz. so much I call my own. I now begin once more to be a woman of property."[3] The counterpoint to this scarcity was the joy of living among her fellow Saints in this, their new Zion. "I feel truly blest of the Lord," she wrote one day, and on another: "This week the Lord has blest me abundantly with strength to

---

1. Snow, Diary, October 31, 1847, in Beecher, *Personal Writings,* 211.
2. Snow, Diary, October 10, 17, 27–28, 1847, in Beecher, *Personal Writings,* 207, 208, 210.
3. Snow, Diary, October 11, 1847, in Beecher, *Personal Writings,* 207.

labor."[4] The women's prayer and blessing meetings that had so refreshed her in Winter Quarters resumed in the valley. She described a meeting of "mothers in Israel" as a "rich treat" and a meeting with younger women as "a time of the outpouring of the spirit of God."[5]

Clarissa Decker Young.

Eliza's first residence in the valley of the Great Salt Lake was in the "Old Fort," a temporary housing complex of some 450 dirt-roofed log cabins spread over thirty acres. There she shared a fourteen-by-sixteen-foot cabin with her sister-wife Clarissa (or Clara) Decker Young, who was one of the three women who had journeyed with the vanguard company that had entered the valley in July. "Have my things put into Clarissa's room, who said Prest. Y[oung] wrote her that I would live with her," Eliza noted in her diary on October 3.[6] At the same time, Clarissa wrote to their husband, Brigham, that "Sister Eliza Snow is coming in the morning to live with me. I was much pleased with the arrangement."[7]

Also living with Clarissa and Eliza for some time was an Indian girl named Sally. The Indians had threatened to kill her if the settlers did not "buy" her and take her to live with them, and Clarissa's brother, Charles Decker, traded his horse and rifle to the Indians in exchange for Sally's life. Eliza and Clarissa were initially put in charge of Sally's housing and education, and Sally continued to live with various members of the

---

4. Snow, Diary, October 20 and November 6, 1847, in Beecher, *Personal Writings,* 209, 211.

5. Snow, Diary, November 2 and 8, in Beecher, *Personal Writings,* 211.

6. Snow, Diary, October 3, 1847, in Beecher, *Personal Writings,* 204; Clara Young to Brigham Young, October 9, 1847, quoted in Beecher, *Personal Writings,* 291–92.

7. Snow, Diary, October 7, 1847, in Beecher, *Personal Writings,* 204; Clara Young to Brigham Young, October 9, 1847, quoted in Beecher, *Personal Writings,* 291–92.

Young family and later married Ute chief Kanosh. "She proved to be a good, virtuous woman, and died beloved by all who knew her," Eliza wrote.[8]

Eliza's only complaint about her accommodations was that "this hut . . . was roofed with willows and earth," with the roof being "nearly flat. We suffered no inconvenience until about the middle of March, when a long storm of snow, sleet, and rain occurred." One night, "despite all discomfitures, I laughed involuntarily while alone in the darkness of the night I lay reflecting the ludicrous scene. The earth over head being fully saturated, after it commenced to drip, the storm was much worse inside than out, and as the water coursed through the willows and patterned on the floor, washed the stones from the earth above, and they went clink, clink, while the numerous mice which the storm had driven in for shelter, ran squealing back and forth."[9]

Clarissa was more than twenty years younger than Eliza, but the two women lived together for nearly a year and formed a strong friendship. When Brigham Young returned from Winter Quarters with other members of his large family in September 1848, housing arrangements were adjusted, and Eliza and Clarissa each moved to other living quarters in the fort. Eliza then spent a brief period in the home of Jonathan and Elvira Holmes, old friends from Nauvoo.

Even makeshift living quarters could seem like home as friends visited and socialized. Eliza recorded one such visit not in her diary but in a poem written to one of her dearest friends, Leonora Cannon Taylor. A native of the Isle of Man, Leonora moved to Canada, where she married John Taylor, who was to become the third

Leonora Cannon Taylor.

---

8. Snow, "Sketch," in Beecher, *Personal Writings,* 30–31. See also George Crane, "Funeral of a Lamanite," *Deseret News [Weekly],* December 18, 1878, 786.

9. Snow, "Sketch," in Beecher, *Personal Writings,* 30–31.

president of the Church. True to British tradition, Leonora loved to garden and was a skilled horticulturalist. In September 1848, she took to Eliza a bouquet of flowers that concealed another gift, a packet of herbs for tea. After Leonora left, Eliza wrote a delightful and whimsical poem of thanks, using her own signature to finish the last line. She first praises Leonora's "patience and toil" and her love of gardening and then continues, remarking first on the flowers:

> *They truly are lovely—I gaze on them oft—*
> *Their fragrance is sweet, their expression is soft;*
> *They have goodness, grace, beauty, and dignity too;*
> *With all these combining, they represent you.*
>
> *Dear Lady, I'm thankful indeed for the flow'rs,*
> *They afford me amusement in my lonely hours;*
> *But for med'cine, there's nothing more welcome to me,*
> *Of the "vain things of earth," than the bundle of Tea.*
>
> *You were sly as a smuggler: I chanc'd to espy*
> *Something hidden, just when you were bidding "good bye":*
> *I might have expos'd it with thanks, but you know,*
> *Good manners prevented.*
>
> ELIZA R. SNOW.[10]

Over time Brigham Young constructed several residences for his wives and children on his property east of the ten-acre square he had designated as the "temple block." He built a row of log dwellings near what is now First Avenue in Salt Lake City, just east of State Street. On Thursday, March 1, 1849, Eliza noted in her diary,

---

10. Stanzas 3–5 of a 5-stanza unpublished poem composed September 7, 1848, John Taylor Collection, Church History Library, The Church of Jesus Christ of Latter-day Saints, Salt Lake City, Utah; hereafter cited as Church History Library. See *Complete Poetry*, 385–86.

"B's folks move out of Fort," and she described in subsequent entries her own gradual move into one of the new Young homes:

"[Friday, April 13, 1849]. . . . Wed. B. Y. come for me to visit his family, which he commenc'd organizing for living together. I spent the night & he took me to Br. [Heber C.] K[imball]'s the next day—told me to go home from there & he should soon come & move me up. He call'd this eve with Loisa, Margaret & Clara. . . .

"[Tuesday, June 19, 1849] This eve. I rode to Prest. Y.s in carriage[.]

"[Thursday, June 21, 1849] return'd home.

"[Thursday, June 28, 1849] Mov'd to Prest. Y.s Log. row[.]"[11]

Eliza's seven years in the Log Row were times of growth and change for the Latter-day Saints and for Eliza personally. Irrigation systems were dug, crops were planted, and homes and other structures were erected, turning the desert wilderness, day by day, into a small, thriving frontier city. Thousands of Latter-day Saints, the fruits of extensive missionary labor, left their homelands to join fellow Church members "in the midst of the snow-cover'd mountains,"[12] establishing a string of settlements along the valleys fronting the Wasatch Mountains, which are part of the extensive Rocky Mountain range.

Salt Lake City, or Great Salt Lake City as it was known during this period, became the center of an increasingly rich cultural life, with a tabernacle for church meetings and a social hall for plays, balls, and concerts. Each public and private building in the spreading city had its place on the grid of streets that extended in the four cardinal directions from the temple block. Four days after he arrived in the valley of the Great Salt Lake in July 1847, Brigham Young designated the site for a new temple and a surrounding ten-acre temple block, now known as Temple Square. It was to be at the heart of the city. For nearly three decades it would also be at the heart of Eliza's life.

---

11. Snow, Diary, March 1, April 13, June 19, 21, and 28, 1849, in Beecher, *Personal Writings*, 227–29.

12. Line from Snow's poem "National Song," composed July 24, 1850, and published in *Poems* (1856). See *Complete Poetry*, 397–98.

The Endowment House in Salt Lake City, about 1880. Photograph by Charles R. Savage.
Eliza served here as often as four days a week.

Eliza had received her temple endowment in Nauvoo in 1845. She would not live to see the Salt Lake Temple dedicated in 1893, but in 1851, even before cornerstones were laid for that temple, Church leaders directed the resumption of temple ordinances in the upper story of the new Council House, the Latter-day Saints' first public building in the Salt Lake Valley.[13] In July 1852, Eliza began to administer temple rites to other women. In May 1855, a separate Endowment House was dedicated on the temple block and Brigham Young appointed Eliza to "take charge of and preside over the women's work therein."[14] She was present at the dedication of that "House of the Lord," as she termed it, describing it as "a privilege that cannot be too highly

13. "Endowment Houses," in Ludlow, *Encyclopedia of Mormonism,* 2:456.

14. Whitney, *History of Utah,* 4:575. Snow's note regarding the Council House and some 1852 dates when she worked there appear on the last page of Nauvoo Relief Society Minutes, 1842–1844, Church History Library. That she administered ordinances in the Council House on this date is corroborated in "Pre-Endowment House Ordinances, 1847–1854," Church History Library.

estimated."[15] She wrote in 1885 that from the time of that 1855 dedication, whenever she was in Salt Lake, she was "a constant officiate in that House."[16] For thirty years Eliza functioned as a central figure in the administration of the endowment for Latter-day Saint women. Her colleague and friend Emmeline B. Wells did not exaggerate when she observed that "thousands of the daughters of Zion, have received blessings under her [Eliza's] hands."[17]

In 1853, Brigham Young presided over the laying of the cornerstones for the Salt Lake Temple. The ceremony included a processional, orations, and prayers. A choir performed an anthem Eliza had written for the occasion, probably to the tune we know today as "Now Let Us Rejoice."[18] The first line refers to the organization of the Church on April 6, 1830, exactly twenty-three years before the celebration.

> *Our Era this day numbers three years and twenty,*
> *And lo! a great people inhabit the West;*
> *The Lord God of Abra'm, the great God of battles,*
> *Who leads forth to vict'ry, appointed our rest.*
>
> *CHORUS.*
> *The Temple, The Temple—we'll build up the Temple,*
> *A court of salvation—iniquity's rod—*
> *A glorious beacon—a light on the mountains—*
> *A portal for angels—a threshold for God.*
>
> *The stones of the corner—the Temple's foundation*
> *In peace, in the City of Brigham are laid;*
> *In the chambers of Israel, the ground that is sacred,*
> *Where righteousness triumphs—where truth is obey'd.*

---

15. Snow, "Sketch," in Beecher, *Personal Writings,* 32.
16. Snow, "Sketch," in Beecher, *Personal Writings,* 32.
17. "Pen Sketch of an Illustrious Woman: Eliza R. Snow Smith," *Woman's Exponent* 9 (February 1, 1881): 131.
18. *Hymns* (1985), no. 3.

> Glad tidings of joy to the spirits in prison,
>> To the Saints of all countries and Isles of the sea,
> For a Temple of God in the midst of the mountains;
>> And joy in the courts of the highest will be.
>
> The Lord whom ye seek will soon come to his Temple,
>> The covenant messenger whom ye desire;
> He'll purify Israel as gold in the furnace,
>> Consuming the dross with unquenchable fire.[19]

By the end of December 1854, Eliza's brother Lorenzo had completed a "large two-story adobe house" on South Temple Street in Salt Lake City and decided to host regular weekly gatherings there with a group of associates he called the Polysophical Society. According to Eliza, these meetings were "a most remarkable combination of physical, moral, mental and spiritual exercises."[20] Friends thus assembled shared their musical, theatrical, and literary talents. Eliza composed and read many poems for this group. She read these lines on January 9, 1855:

> My Brothers and Sisters, I'm happy to be
> Where the atmosphere's pure—where the spirit is free—
> Where clear rays from the light of Eternity shine—
> Where reflections from Intellect's luminous mine
> Brightly beam from each eye—in each countenance glow—
> Where pure currents of thought, unobstructedly flow—
> Where sweet singers and players, rich off'rings impart
> To form telegraph lines from the head to the heart.[21]

---

19. Stanzas 1–4 and 6 of "The Temple," 7-stanza hymn. See *Complete Poetry,* 444–46.
20. Snow, *Biography and Family Record,* 236.
21. Lines 1–8 of a 72-line poem originally titled "Address" and published in *Deseret News,* January 18, 1855. See *Complete Poetry,* 469–72.

Three weeks later, her topic for the Polysophical Society was "Woman." Her poetic address included these lines:

> Let woman then, a course in life pursue
> To purchase man's respect, as merit's due,
> And feeling God's approval, act her part
> With noble independence in her heart;
>
> Nor change, nor swerve, nor shrink, whatever is;
> Though fools may scoff—impertinence may quiz:
> Faithful, though oft in faithfulness unknown—
> With no whereon to lean, but God alone.
>
> Queen of her household—authorized to bless—
> To plant the principles of righteousness. . . .
> And thro' obedience woman will obtain
> The power of reigning and the right to reign.[22]

This and other poems show that Eliza was aware of contemporary questions surrounding the status of women. On the national scene, woman's rights activists, who had first gathered at Seneca Falls in 1848, had begun to campaign for educational opportunities, political and economic power, and for women's suffrage. In 1852, Eliza conceded the existing dominant role of men, inviting the "female conventionists" to come to Utah, where they might find "noble men / Whom they'll be proud t' acknowledge to be far / Their own superiors."[23] By the time she addressed the Polysophical Society, however, she chose to speak of the eternal worth and destiny of women, not by claiming the superiority of either sex but by reminding the audience

---

22. Lines 69–76, 121–22, and 137–38 of "Woman," a 138-line poem published in *The Mormon* (December 27, 1856): [1]. See *Complete Poetry*, 474–79.

23. Lines 73 and 76–78 from "The New Year 1852," a 95-line poem published in *Deseret News*, January 10, 1852. See *Complete Poetry*, 419–23.

Lion House, left, and Beehive House, right, 1880; photograph by Charles W. Carter.

that a woman is not a "play-thing" or a "dazzling butterfly" but one with a "holy call-ing," holding with man "a key / Of present and eternal destiny."[24]

In 1856, nine years after her arrival in the Salt Lake Valley, Eliza moved to the re-cently completed three-story Lion House, where she maintained a small but comfort-able room of her own until her death more than thirty years later. Here, among the extended family of Brigham Young, she continued to enjoy not only a secure home but love and fellowship. She was also to find abundant fulfillment of a fervent prayer she had noted in her trail journal: "O Lord my God I pray . . . that I may be useful."[25]

Her days were full and her duties were many. Although there is no Eliza Snow diary after 1849, we can piece together a portion of her associations with family and friends from their records: she sometimes sewed at a quilting, sometimes stayed through the night with friends to minister to a dying child. "She was as faithful at the bedside of

---

24. "Woman," 41–43, 45–46.

25. Snow, Diary, June 24, 1846, in Beecher, *Personal Writings*, 137.

OPPOSITE: *Eliza's embroidery of a lion is a detail from the Twentieth Ward album quilt (also shown). Photograph of the Lion House and Beehive House, 1860, by Marsena Cannon.*

sickness as even aunt Zina [Huntington Young] could be and her cool hand laid upon the fevered brow of a fevered child was like a heavenly benediction," Brigham's daughter Susa Young Gates remembered. Eliza was also a reader: "She spent all of her spare time in study of great and good books, beginning with the Bible and Book of Mormon, with which she was intimately familiar, and ending with the classics of the ages past." Susa noted also that "to relieve the nervous pressure of too much study, [Eliza] embroidered temple aprons or made burial clothing. . . . Her embroideries were real works of art."[26]

And she continued to write poetry. Eliza composed verses to mark virtually every public occasion. Her poems celebrated the Typographical Association of Deseret, the planning of the railroad, local and national holidays, and other special events. And like a nation's poet laureate, she wrote more serious poetry representing her people's beliefs, experiences, and culture. As the Latter-day Saint communities expanded, new forums emerged for her writings. Elaborate celebrations for the Fourth and Twenty-Fourth of July were inaugurated and she "was expected to furnish one song, and sometimes more than one, for each of these occasions."[27] When the *Deseret News* began publication in June 1850, she became a frequent contributor. She composed hymn texts for Church hymnals published in 1851 and 1856. Eliza's words helped shape the Saints' understanding of what the community and its citizens might become. Indeed, it was during these years that Eliza Snow began to be known as "Zion's Poetess." "Zion's welfare is my portion," she wrote.[28] Whether paying tribute to leaders and missionaries, bearing fervent testimony of the restored gospel, or rejoicing in a community building or gathering, she cherished Zion. And she often wielded her pen in Zion's defense.

Eliza wrote a wonderful little poem, undated and unpublished, that expressed her feelings about her mission as a poet. It is a response to someone—his identity is unknown—who had offered to pay her to write a poem. After all, some of Eliza's

---

26. "Life in the Lion House," Susa Young Gates Collection, Box 12, fd. 2, p. 40, Utah State Historical Society, Salt Lake City.

27. Snow, "Sketch," in Beecher, *Personal Writings*, 33.

28. Line 9 of "All Is Well," a 20-line poem published in Snow's *Poems* (1856). See *Complete Poetry*, 527–28.

contemporaries, such as the popular Lydia H. Sigourney, made a living by writing and publishing poems. Eliza, however, replied to the request with these scornful lines:

> You "pay the Poet," Sir, you say—
> > Permit me to inquire,
> What Inspiration prompts the lay
> > When Poets write for hire?
>
> My lyre, when circumstance approves,
> > Is prompt to friendship's call:
> I have a pen that <u>freely</u> moves,
> > Or does <u>not</u> <u>move</u> <u>at</u> <u>all</u>.[29]

Note the double connotation of the word *freely*. Her pen is free in the sense of being unpaid and is thus free to express honest thought.

Although Eliza became known as "Zion's Poetess," she was not selfish about this title. She always welcomed other poets, young and old, who wished to serve the cause of the kingdom. Often she exchanged poems with other writers of verse, Lyman Littlefield, Hannah Tapfield King, and Sarah Elizabeth Carmichael among them. One poem in *Poems 1* shows her generosity of spirit in celebrating the talents of a fellow poet. In 1853, Scottish convert John Lyon published an anthology of poetry called *Harp of Zion*. He sent Eliza a copy of the volume, which included a poem by Lyon himself beginning "Eliza Snow is the queen of the muse." She responded to the gift and the compliment with a poem in his honor. Her poem concludes with this praise of Lyon's work:

> I accept the fair gift, the rich, beautiful boon,
> > With gratitude mingled with pleasure:

---

29. Stanzas 1 and 3 of a 3-stanza poem titled simply "To———." The poem is recorded in Snow, Journal, 1842 to 1882, Church History Library. See *Complete Poetry*, 261; underlining in original.

With its heaven-inspir'd pages I love to commune,
And, possessing it, feel I've a treasure.[30]

Eliza's first volume of *Poems: Religious, Historical, and Political,* published under Church auspices in Liverpool, England, in 1856, featured poems she had written between 1838 and 1854. As the title of the volume indicates, these poems address many different subjects and embody many moods. Some of them encouraged individual missionaries, honored Church leaders, or marked many historical occasions, such as the Twenty-Fourth of July; several were addressed to Joseph Smith or were about him, including "Two Chapters of the Life of Joseph Smith"; others were contemplative: "Saturday Evening Thoughts," "Apostrophe to Death," "As I Believe."

Most of the verses in *Poems 1,* many of them historical, followed a chronological order; however, the first poem following the dedication was "O My Father," titled in this volume "Invocation, or the Eternal Father and Mother." A decade after it was written, the hymn text remained a particular favorite of Brigham Young and of Eliza herself. For more than 150 years, prophets and Saints have prized the simple eloquence with which "O My Father" captures some of the most profound truths of the gospel.

Poems 1, *published in 1856.*

---

30. Stanza 3 of a 3-stanza poem written about 1853 and published in *Poems* (1856). See *Complete Poetry,* 451; emphasis in original.

Always alert for ways in which she could support the Church's vast missionary effort, Eliza wrote a missionary hymn for the 1851 hymnal. Before that time, missionary work had not been a widespread theme in the Church's hymnody, but with the missionaries' ongoing success in the British Isles and the productive Scandinavian Mission having been organized in 1850, the Church obviously needed and enjoyed such hymns. Eliza's hymn, still popular today, is "The Time Is Far Spent."[31] Following is the first stanza:

> The time is far spent—there is little remaining,
> To publish glad tidings, by sea and by land,
> Then hasten, ye heralds! go forward proclaiming,
> Repent for the Kingdom of Heaven's at hand.[32]

Besides poems encouraging the missionary "heralds" in their work in many nations, Eliza wrote poems to individual missionaries. Wilford Woodruff Jr., born while his father was serving a mission in England, was the son of two of Eliza's closest friends, Phebe Wittemore Carter Woodruff and Wilford Woodruff Sr. In April 1863, Wilford Jr. accepted his own mission call to England. She wrote these lines of encouragement to him while he was on his mission:

> God bless you, young brother and fill you with light—
> Endow you with wisdom and clothe you with might—
> Give pow'rs of discernment and ever bestow
> What skill will be needful to thwart every foe.
>
> God bless you, young Brother, wherever you are
> And help you with boldness the Gospel declare:
> Fill your mission with honor then joyfully come
> And bless with your presence your friends and your home.[33]

---

31. *Hymns* (1985), no. 266.

32. Of Snow's 6 original stanzas, 4 are in *Hymns* (1985), no. 266. See *Complete Poetry*, 415–16.

33. Stanzas 1 and 6 of an unpublished 6-stanza poem composed April 22, 1864, and recorded in Snow's

Then, when young Wilford returned from his mission in 1866, Eliza wrote words for his fifteen-year-old sister Bulah (or Beulah) to sing at his homecoming celebration. Eliza instructed that the words, with the refrain "Willie is at home again," were to be sung to a popular tune of the time, "Jamie's on the Stormy Sea":

> *While with love's warm hand we press him—*
> *With affection's tones caress him*
> *And in truth's bold accents bless him*
>   *Fondly we repeat the strain*
>
> *Of all other strains most cheering—*
> *Sound of sounds the most endearing*
> *Thro' time's vista brightly peering*
>   <u>*Willie is at home again*</u>.[34]

Brigham Young believed that "every pure enjoyment was from heaven and was for the Saints,"[35] and his people moved quickly to build a cultural life in Salt Lake City. The fifteen-hundred-seat Salt Lake Theater, largely completed in December 1861, was the scene of plays, musical theater, and more formal concerts. The theater was a public works project, as were the new tabernacle, commenced in 1863, and the great temple, whose new fifteen-foot-wide foundation of local granite neared ground level in 1865.

Other developments were not as welcome. Although the first decade in the valley was a time of relative peace for the Latter-day Saints, they were repeatedly thwarted in their intention to establish their own distinctive government, one in which ecclesiastical and civil authority merged, according to the pattern established by Joseph Smith in Nauvoo. The Territory of Utah was created as part of the Compromise of 1850, and Latter-day Saints struggled for the next half-century against the federal government's

---

Journal, 1842–1882. See *Complete Poetry*, 667–68.

34. Stanza 4 of an unpublished 4-stanza song recorded in Snow, Journal, 1842–1882. See *Complete Poetry*, 734–35; underlining in original.

35. Quoted in Pyper, *Romance of an Old Playhouse*, 97.

involvement in territorial affairs. In 1852, the first public acknowledgment of plural marriage gave rise to much criticism, particularly of Mormon women, and triggered repeated attempts by the United States Congress to pass "anti-polygamy" legislation aimed at terminating the practice. Eliza cherished Zion as a bastion of liberty and justice—"Where have the Constitution and laws reigned during the last few years, but in Utah?" she asked in 1858—and she did not hesitate to criticize, sometimes bitterly, governmental attempts to interfere with Saints' regulation of their own society.[36]

"That 'men are born poets' is a common adage—I was born a patriot,"[37] Eliza proudly declared. In her childhood, she had heard her grandfather Oliver Snow recount his part in the American Revolution and she had grown up with a love for her country. Although the Saints had fled the United States to seek refuge in the Rocky Mountains, Eliza, like other American Saints, considered herself a loyal citizen of her country. She wrote after seeing a "grand display of flags":

> *I love that Flag.—When in my childish glee—*
> *A prattling girl upon my grand-sire's knee;*
> *I heard him tell strange tales, with valor rife,*
> *How that same Flag was bought with blood and life:*
> *And his tall form, seem'd taller, when he said*
> *"Child, for that Flag, your grandpa fought and bled:"*
> *My young heart felt that every scar he wore,*
> *Caused him to prize that banner, more and more.*
>
> *I caught the fire, and as in years I grew,*
> *I loved the Flag—I loved my country too.*
> *My bosom swell'd with pride, to think my birth*
> *Was on that highly favored spot of Earth.*

---

36. Snow's footnote to a poem published in *Deseret News,* September 1, 1858. See *Complete Poetry,* 574–75.

37. Snow, "Sketch," in Beecher, *Personal Writings,* 8.

> *There came a time, which I remember well,*
>
> *Beneath the Stars and Stripes, we could not dwell!*
>
> *We had to flee; but in our hasty flight,*
>
> *We grasped the Flag, with more than mortal might;*
>
> *And vow'd although our foes should us bereave*
>
> *Of all things else, the Flag we would not leave.*
>
> *We took the Flag, and journeying to the West,*
>
> *We wore its motto graven on each breast.*
>
> *Here we arrived in peace, and God be praised,*
>
> *Anon our Country's glorious standard raised;*
>
> *And the dear Flag, in graceful majesty,*
>
> *Hail'd to the mountains, Union—Liberty.*[38]

Her deep love of country fired Eliza's emotions during the years that include the Utah War, 1857–58, and the American Civil War, 1861–65. After the designation of Utah as a United States territory in 1850, tensions escalated between Church leaders and the federal territorial appointees who criticized and sought to undermine the leadership of Brigham Young, appointed first governor of the Territory of Utah. In the summer of 1857, President James Buchanan ordered federal troops to Utah Territory to quell a supposed "Mormon rebellion" and replace Brigham Young as governor. Fearing a renewal of the violence the Saints had experienced in Missouri and Illinois, President Young (who also served as governor) declared martial law in September 1857. Between March and May 1858, under his instruction, some thirty thousand Saints living in Salt Lake and the surrounding area evacuated their homes. With the rest of Brigham's family, Eliza moved south to Utah Valley, where they remained until the

---

38. Lines 1–24 of a 46-line poem, "My Own, My Country's Flag: Lines Suggested by the Grand Display of Flags in Honor of the Re-inauguration of President Lincoln," published in *Deseret News,* March 15, 1865. See *Complete Poetry,* 685–87.

Johnston's Army marching through Salt Lake City.

end of June. On June 26, fifty-five hundred federal troops marched across the Salt Lake Valley. They soon established Camp Floyd, forty-five miles southwest of Salt Lake City.

A new governor was peacefully installed and the Utah War ended in the summer of 1858. Eliza and other Saints returned to their homes, but their place of refuge had permanently changed. Army troops remained stationed at Camp Floyd for the next three years, with attendant camp followers, teamsters, and suppliers. The territory's population of non-Mormons continued to increase. In the eyes of the Saints, many of the "Gentiles"—a term for those who were not Latter-day Saints—contributed to licentious influences in Salt Lake City.

In a mocking, indignant poem she wrote two years after the end of the Utah War, titled "The Fathers—Wouldn't They Be Astonished?" Eliza asked what the Founding Fathers of the United States would think if they could see what had become of the nation's Congress:

> *Could they get one full expression*
> *Of our Congress' present session—*
> *Could they take one single peep in,*
> *They would surely fall to weeping.*

They would weep and blush and wonder
At the noisy wind and thunder—
At the boisterous, wrathy prattle—
At the steam and tittle tattle—

Could our Washington and Adams,
Jefferson and other sages,
Look upon the present scenery,
With its underwire machinery—
All the multiform dissentions
Of the multiplied conventions;
Some intent on office seeking—
Some intent on money eking—
All mix'd up in twists and jangles,
All absorb'd in wordy wrangles.

If they look for "Rights" as equal,
As they hop'd for in the sequel
Of their hardships and privations—
Of their wise deliberations,
When the government they founded—
When the trump of peace they sounded;
They would think their labors wasted
And the fruits thereof, untasted—
That altho' their deeds are boasted,
And their names on way-marks posted;
They are virtually forgotten,
And the Constitution rotten.[39]

---

39. Lines 7–14, 17–26, and 45–56 of an undated 56-line poem published in Snow's *Poems* (1877). See *Complete Poetry*, 616–18.

The frustration Eliza expressed in this 1860 poem reflected the escalating conflicts about to devastate the nation she loved. The American Civil War commenced in April 1861. Although Latter-day Saints in Utah Territory were geographically separated from the horrific battles between North and South, they felt the war's impact. In her Fourth of July and other poems, Eliza expressed sorrow at the fratricide. She and other Latter-day Saints struggled with profound disillusionment with their country. In Missouri, Illinois, and now in Utah Territory, state and federal officials had failed to protect Saints' lives, rights, and property. Maintaining hope in the nation's founding ideals, Eliza came to see the Saints as the true guardians of peace and liberty in a time of national bloodshed:

> Fight on, if fight you will: At length
> > The North and South, alike will feel,
> With all their boast, in martial strength,
> > Protection is not made of steel.
> Here, without bloodshed, is maintain'd
> > The freedom patriots prize most dear.
> Not "might," but Truth and Right have gain'd
> > In peace a "glorious triumph" here.[40]

Against this backdrop of war, Eliza valued the blessing of living in peace in Zion. She rallied the Saints by reaffirming the most basic truths and reminding them of what they stood for as a people. For the rest of her life, as she continued to proclaim the sanctity of liberty and of the United States Constitution, she celebrated the distinctive Mormon culture developing in the Great Basin: a covenant community with a temple at its center, led by prophets of God, interconnected by extended family and ecclesiastical networks, and replenished by outgoing missionaries, incoming immigrants, and multiplying wards and villages. Eliza proclaimed the Saints, with their

---

40. Lines 49–56 of a 60-line poem written to William Cullen Bryant as a response to his poem "Our Country's Call." See *Complete Poetry*, 626–28.

peculiar blend of theocracy and democracy, to be the "saving remnant," offering to a fractured nation the promise of "Liberty, Peace, and Salvation."[41]

The peace Eliza felt in her "home in the west" stemmed from her continuing faith in the restored gospel of Christ and her understanding of it, as well as from her connections to the Saints in Zion.[42] Indeed, her devotion to the restored gospel seems interwoven with her love for the Saints who were engaged in building Zion. Her warm feelings for friends and family, and theirs for her, sustained her over the years, and she often wrote of the power of such love to bless the human family. She wrote to a friend, "I think there is no possible danger of you loving [your baby daughter] too much. . . . The idea of our loving innocent beings too much, is, I think, a mistaken one—it belongs to sectarianism and not to pure christianity."[43]

Family ties are eternal—this Eliza knew from the teachings of Joseph Smith. In addition, she cherished the view that the ties of friendship, as well as those of family, were also an enduring, eternal blessing. In the autograph book of Sarah Melissa Granger Kimball, a dear friend who had participated with Eliza in the founding of the Female Relief Society of Nauvoo, she wrote these sensitive lines:

The cords of fellowship that bind
Heart unto heart and mind to mind;
Innately form'd, entwining fast
In noble natures, ever last.

Those who celestial laws abide,
Who by those laws are purified;

41. The phrase "Liberty, Peace, and Salvation" is from "Song for the 24th of July, 1857," line 4. See *Complete Poetry*, 554–56.
42. Line 6 of "To the Saints in Europe," a poem composed April 20, 1852, and published in *Millennial Star*, October 16, 1852. See *Complete Poetry*, 425–26.
43. Eliza R. Snow to Rhoda Ann Richards, July 29, 1863, S. Norman Lee Papers, Photocopy and typed transcription of manuscript, L. Tom Perry Special Collections, Harold B. Lee Library, Brigham Young University, Provo, Utah.

Will be in love and union one,
As God the Father and the Son.[44]

The bonds of love and friendship that Eliza had established in Ohio, Missouri, and Nauvoo held fast in the Salt Lake Valley. In 1858, she addressed a poem to George W. Pitkin, who had been her friend from her childhood in Ohio through the westward exodus of the Saints. Contrary to Brigham Young's counsel to avoid the gold fields, George and his family had left Utah Territory for three years in search of gold in California and Oregon. Eventually the Pitkins returned to Salt Lake City. Eliza's nonjudgmental poem, written as a personal letter to George Pitkin, affirms their enduring friendship and lends love and encouragement. "Fear not the future nor regret the past," she advised. George, she testified, is "a God in embryo," gaining knowledge by experience "for usefulness in an exalted sphere." She continued by reminding him that the Lord not only is willing to forgive our errors but can sanctify them to our future wisdom:

Thus, oft through human erring, good proceeds,
As wisdom's earnings for our future needs—
Thus God, to you, the past will sanctify
And in your heart will wisdom multiply;
And from your life its volumes yet will flow,
And to your kindred words of life bestow.[45]

Many of Eliza's poems to her friends were written as encouragement in times of trial. When one of Eliza's friends suffered the death of a loved one—the kind of loss that she once described as "nature's tithing of the heart"—she was quick to offer a poem of consolation.[46] In Nauvoo, Eliza had heard Joseph Smith declare the doctrine

---

44. These lines composed in 1852 were unpublished. See *Complete Poetry,* 437.

45. Lines 35, 42, and 43–48 of a 54-line unpublished poem. See *Complete Poetry,* 577–79.

46. Line 4 of "A Tribute to the Memory of Mr. Cooke," published in *Deseret News,* May 6, 1863. See *Complete Poetry,* 649–50.

that has comforted the heart of many a grief-stricken mother: "'Will mothers have their children in eternity?' Yes! Yes! Mothers, you shall have your children; for they shall have eternal life, for their debt is paid . . . it will still be the child, in the same precise form [when it rises] as it appeared before it died out of its mother's arms."[47] Charles and Sarah Loveless Wight, friends Eliza knew in Brigham City, lost three daughters in infancy. Eliza's poem on the death of their daughter Ann Eliza, who died before she was two months old, was later published as a hymn text with a tune by Ebenezer Beesley. The text continued in Latter-day Saint hymnody until 1927.[48] Following are two stanzas from Eliza's poem:

> *Your sweet little rose bud has left you*
> *To bloom in a holier sphere:*
> *He that gave it, in wisdom bereft you;*
> *Then why should you cherish a tear?*

> *Your babe in the grave is not sleeping,*
> *She has joined her dear sisters above;*
> *Bright beings now have them in keeping*
> *In a mansion of beauty and love.*[49]

In September 1864, in company with Brigham Young and other Church leaders, Eliza traveled to southern Utah Territory, the land known among the Latter-day Saints as Dixie, for a four-week visit. More than three hundred families had been called to settle the region in 1861, and other families had joined them since that time. During this visit, Brigham Young encouraged the settlers in their struggle against Dixie's desert climate and unyielding soil. After she returned to Salt Lake City, Eliza

---

47. See Smith, *History of the Church,* 6:316.
48. Beesley's tune continues as the setting for the hymn "Let Us Oft Speak Kind Words," *Hymns* (1985), no. 232.
49. Stanzas 1 and 2 of a 5-stanza poem published in *Deseret News,* August 10, 1859. See *Complete Poetry,* 588–89.

Dixie Homesteaders, *by Glen Hopkinson.*

expressed her admiration for the landscape and its settlers, and she echoed Brigham's words of encouragement to the Dixie Saints as they reclaimed the desert lands:

> *I love the land of Dixie—*
> *Our mountain Dixie land;*
> *Where peace is in the atmosphere,*
> *And wealth amid the sand.*
>
> *Success to loyal Dixie,*
> *Fair Utah's sunny land;*
> *Where faith and industry will soon,*
> *A mass of wealth command.*[50]

During this trip, Eliza was able to renew many friendships, including her close relationship with Hannah Gould Perkins, an educated English convert who with her husband had left Salt Lake City in 1861 to settle St. George. Aware of the immense struggle and hard labor of the Dixie Saints, Eliza later wrote to Hannah, "I daily think

---

50. Lines 1–4 and 53–56 of a 60-line poem published in *Deseret News,* October 26, 1864. See *Complete Poetry,* 676–78.

of the very hard work you are all doing—I know you never could perform it if you did not live near to the Lord."[51]

The Saints living in the Salt Lake Valley, Dixie, and other Mormon settlements in Utah Territory had gathered from many parts of the United States, the British Isles, and Scandinavia. Some were new converts; some had been members for decades. Though the Saints differed in their backgrounds, nationalities, languages, and customs, they were united in their beliefs. A poem Eliza read before the Polysophical Society was called "Nationality." She explained to the audience,

> *I do not languish for the lakes and rills—*
> *The rugged heights of Europe's Alpine hills—*
> *The verdant vales which beauteously repose*
> *'Neath their bold summits of eternal snows.*
> *Nor would I boast a proud nativity—*
> *On the luxuriant plains of Italy,*
> *With glowing, sunny landscapes, rich and fair—*
> *Tall city spires and grand cathedrals there.*

She went on to mention Germany, Britain, Sweden, Norway, and France, describing their beauties but pointing out that no matter how fond we are of our homeland,

> *The Holy Spirit, ev'ry saint receives*
> *Is one sense added to what nature gives;*
> *Instructed by this spirit-sense, we learn,*
> *More than corporeal senses can discern.*
> *It sees we are not natives of this earth—*
> *We've liv'd before—we had an earlier birth.*
> *As foreign trav'lers, each a camping ground*
> *On diff'rent portions of the earth have found;*

---

51. Eliza R. Snow to Hannah Gould Perkins, October 12, 1862, Church History Library.

The force of habit gives to each, a grace—
Peculiar charms to each and ev'ry place:
And yet, with all the adoration felt
As at their shrines devotedly we knelt,
Not one—not all possess sufficient worth
To make us feel quite nat'ralized to earth.
Our hearts beat upward and our spirits move
In homeward currents, towards those we love.[52]

Eliza felt enriched by living among a community of diverse believers, connected by covenant to the same hopes for eternity. Everyone, no matter from what homeland, is a "foreign trav'ler," merely "camping" on this earth. Our true home, Eliza affirmed, is "Eternity."

---

52. Lines 24–31, 100–101, 106–9, and 120–29 of a 137-line poem published in *Deseret News,* June 26, 1856. See *Complete Poetry,* 486–90.

A postcard view of the Lion House.

Chapter Six

Change on the Heels of Change

1866–1873

In July 1867, as Latter-day Saints celebrated the twentieth anniversary of the arrival of the pioneers in the Salt Lake Valley, Eliza and her associates could look back on an incredible two decades. They were justifiably proud of having tamed the wilderness and built a remarkable city. At the request of her close friend Bathsheba Smith and to commemorate the Twenty-Fourth of July (Pioneer Day) in 1867, Eliza wrote a poem titled "Twenty Years Ago." As she rolled back "the curtain of the past," she contrasted the snakes, crickets, and "barren sod" Saints encountered in 1847 with the "merry glee" and "richest gifts" of their present home in the Valley:

Twenty Years Ago

Beneath the mountains crown'd with snows,
With future prospects rife:
The desert blossoms as the rose,
And teems with joyous life.
Roll back the curtain of the past
Where time's swift changes flow,
And take a retrospective cast
Of twenty years ago.

In summer's sunshine, crickets here,
And snakes, their rights maintain'd;
And o'er the winters, bleak and drear,
Cold desolation reign'd.
Let fall the curtain—look and see
The present bright tableau,
Contrasted with the scenery
Of twenty years ago.[1]

In 1867 Eliza was sixty-three years old. As she spent time with friends like Bathsheba, she considered how change marked their shared past and what it might mean to their shared future. At the end of 1867, she wrote these lines: "'Tis the evening of Time, and it is not strange / That Change should tread on the heels of Change."[2] The transcontinental telegraph had been completed in 1864 and the great transcontinental railroad was under construction, whittling away at the Saints' isolation in the Great Basin. As they felt the increasing press of influences from the outside world, Latter-day Saints sought to maintain their sense of identity and solidarity as a religious community. They doubled their missionary force, encouraged emigration, emphasized economic cooperation, and elaborated the Church organization. Eliza supported all of these efforts through her poetry, and she soon found additional channels for her commitment. Brigham Young appointed her to take a leading part in the 1867–68 reestablishment of the women's Relief Society and then, two years later, in the establishment of a new organization for younger women. She probably did not imagine how dramatically these assignments would change her life. She was to become widely known as a powerful speaker and vigorous leader, and she would travel widely, even to Europe and the Holy Land, as a spokeswoman and leader of the women of Zion.

---

1. Stanzas 1 and 3 of a 5-stanza poem published in *Deseret News,* July 31, 1867. See *Complete Poetry,* 756–58.
2. Lines 1 and 2 of "Change," a 68-line poem published in *Deseret News,* December 18, 1867. See *Complete Poetry,* 770–72.

As she assumed this significant and visible role in building the Lord's kingdom, Eliza repeatedly expressed gratitude and humility. Perhaps she had sensed an expanded assignment was coming. In 1866 she published a poem in the *Deseret News* called "The Ship," comparing Zion to a ship on the high seas. She warned the passengers—her fellow Saints—that

> *There's no cabin passage on Zion's Ship—*
> *It was never design'd for a pleasure trip—*
> *'Tis an expedition of work, work, work,*
> *With no badges of honor for them that shirk.*[3]

To Eliza, being a Saint meant laboring for Zion, and she was prepared to accept her increasing labors wholeheartedly.

By 1866 Eliza had lived in the Lion House for ten years, establishing for herself a place of respect and honor in the large and active household of Brigham Young. She was close to her sister-wives and to their children, and she continued to treasure relationships with the children of her sister Leonora and her brother Lorenzo. Although she had no sons and daughters of her own, children were very much part of her life and she was ever ready to contribute to their upbringing and well-being. Because she had taught school in Kirtland and Nauvoo and the cause of children's education was close to her heart, Eliza must have welcomed the new *Juvenile Instructor,* a magazine published twice monthly beginning in 1866. Two years earlier, its editor, George Q. Cannon, had launched a movement to revive Sunday schools in Salt Lake City congregations, the first of several organizations to be implemented at the ward level over the next few years. Printed for the Sunday schools, the *Juvenile Instructor* provided a new audience for Eliza's poetry—the children of Zion. Over the next few years, she wrote some twenty-five poems for her young readers. One of them, to be sung to the tune of the popular Civil War song "Tramp, Tramp, Tramp," combines praise and

---

3. Lines 31–34 of a 52-line poem published in *Deseret News,* April 19, 1866. See *Complete Poetry,* 715–17.

encouragement—the children are "generous and brave"—with reminders about good behavior. The song, "In Our Lovely Deseret," is still a favorite today:[4]

In our lovely Deseret, where the saints of God have met,
      There's a multitude of children all around:
They are generous and brave—they have precious souls to save
      They must listen, and obey the gospel sound.

      CHORUS.

Hark! hark! hark! 'Tis children's music
      Children's voices, O how sweet
When in innocence and love, like the angels up above,
      They, with happy hearts, and cheerful faces meet.

That the children may live long, and be beautiful and strong
      Tea and coffee and tobacco, they despise.
Drink no liquor and they eat but a very little meat:
      They are seeking to be great and good and wise.

They should be instructed young, how to watch and guard the tongue,
      And their tempers train, and evil passions bind:
They should always be polite and treat everybody right,
      And in every place be affable and kind.

They must not forget to pray, night and morning, every day,
      For the Lord to keep them safe from every ill
And assist them to do right, that with all their mind and might
      They may love Him, and may learn to do His will.[5]

---

4. *Hymns* (1985), no. 307.

5. This is the entire poem. It was published in *Juvenile Instructor*, November 1, 1867. See *Complete Poetry*, 766–68.

Eliza continued to write poems to comfort parents whose children had died. Several poems regarding the death of children appeared in the *Juvenile Instructor*, including one she wrote after a severe winter in Utah Territory that resulted in much childhood disease and death. We may not be comfortable with the thought of angels coaxing a dying child to hasten to them, but perhaps she knew that at that time both parents and children would be reassured by her depiction of a joyful angelic welcome in heaven. It is one of her most unusual and artful poems, almost mesmerizing in its otherworldly persuasion:

Angel Whisperings to the Dying Child

> *Darling, we are waiting for thee,*
> *Hasten, now:*
> *Go with us, where wreaths are twining*
> *For thy brow.*
>
> *In the innocence of childhood,*
> *Thou wilt be*
> *Hail'd with gentle shouts of welcome,*
> *And of glee.*
>
> *Joyous cherubs wait thy coming*
> *Up above;*
> *Ready now to crown and bless thee,*
> *With their love.*
>
> *Loved one, haste—delay no longer—*
> *With us go*
> *From a clime that intermingles*
> *Joy and woe.*
>
> *Go with us to heav'nly arbors,*
> *Deck'd with flow'rs;*

Where ambrosial fragrance, streaming,
Fills the bow'rs.

Thou art pure—by earth's corruptions
Undefiled;
From the ills of life, we'll take thee,
Sinless child.

Friends will mourn, but this bereavement
They'll endure;
Knowing that their cherished darling
Is secure.

Like a rosebud yet unopen'd,
Thou shalt bloom;
Where no blight shall mar thy freshness,
And perfume.

Child, we're waiting now to bear thee
To our home,
Full of life—of love and beauty,
Darling, come.[6]

Within the Young family and in the families of her siblings and close friends, Eliza R. Snow was known as "Aunt Eliza." She witnessed new generations born and children grow to adulthood. She nursed sick children back to health and dressed for burial those who died. When the children were small, she often signed their autograph books; when they became young adults, she continued to be part of their lives. She wrote several letters to Louisa "Lula" Greene (later Richards), a niece of Brigham Young, whom she usually addressed as "My dear niece." Lula had been disappointed

6. This is the entire poem. It was published in *Juvenile Instructor,* March 13, 1869. The introduction to this poem in *Complete Poetry,* 791–93, gives more information concerning the death of infants.

when a seemingly promising romance had faded away without leading to marriage. Eliza wrote comforting words to her, pointing out that the opportunity to love and teach children was still hers, whether she was married or remained single: "While unmarried, one cannot be fulfilling the requisition of maternity, but let me ask: Is it not as important that those already born should be cultivated and reared for use in the kingdom of God, as that others should be born?"[7]

Similarly, "Aunt Eliza" sought to nurture other young women and young men. Brigham Kimball, son of her friends Vilate and Heber C. Kimball, received a letter from Eliza while serving a mission in England. She knew just how to cheer and encourage him with some half-teasing remarks that communicated her affection and reassurance: "I remember you hinted something about girls all getting married before you return—now I wish to set your heart at rest on this subject. I have a number of pretty nieces—they will not *all* be married. I never so much wished that I had a few daughters of my own—I assure you I would hold one in reserve."[8]

Many of Brigham Young's sons and daughters grew up in the Lion House with Aunt Eliza and remembered her with respect and affection. Susa Young Gates, daughter of Brigham and Lucy Bigelow Young, described Eliza as "eloquent, exquisitely high-principled." The Young daughters were always welcome in Eliza's room, she recalled, "although they did not go as often as might have been good for them; for dear Aunt Eliza's homilies were not always relished by the high-spirited girls who loved fun and frolic with a normal healthy zest."[9]

Clarissa Young Spencer, the youngest daughter of Brigham and Lucy Ann Decker Young, wrote: "No one at the house appealed to me more greatly than Aunt Eliza R. Snow. . . . . She was slight and fragile and always immaculate in dress. I see her now in

---

7. Eliza R. Snow to Louisa Lula Greene Richards, April 23, 1871, Louisa Lula Greene Richards Papers, ca. 1860–1935, Church History Library, The Church of Jesus Christ of Latter-day Saints, Salt Lake City, Utah; hereafter cited as Church History Library.

8. Eliza R. Snow to Brigham Kimball, April 20, 1866; published in *Relief Society Magazine,* January 1918, 6.

9. "Life in the Lion House," Susa Young Gates Collection, Box 12, fd. 2, 39, Utah State Historical Society, Salt Lake City.

her full-skirted, lace-trimmed silk dresses, with her dainty lace caps and a gold chain around her neck, looking for all the world like a piece of Dresden china. She always sat on Father's right at the dinner table and also in the prayer room. He valued her opinion greatly and gave her many important commissions, especially in relation to the women's organizations of the Church."[10]

Eliza received a new commission from Brigham Young in the spring of 1868. It had been thirteen years since he had called her to preside over women's ordinance work in the Endowment House (precursor to the temple in Salt Lake City). In that position, in the extensive Young household, and in her role as Zion's Poetess, she had earned his trust. Further, she was a link to the Prophet Joseph: she had been sealed to him in marriage, had learned gospel truths from him personally, and had recorded and preserved his addresses to the Female Relief Society of Nauvoo. These experiences prepared her for new responsibilities, as she briefly explained when she recounted the circumstances of her new calling: "As I had been intimately associated with, and had officiated as Secretary for the first [Relief Society] organization, Pres. Young commissioned me to assist the Bishops in organizing Branches of the Society in their respective Wards; for, at that time, the Bishops had not acquainted themselves with the movement, and did not know how to proceed. To me it was quite a mission, and I took much pleasure in its performance."[11] Thus Eliza began the administrative work that would occupy her for the final two decades of her life.

She began by visiting ward after ward throughout Utah Territory, often reading Joseph Smith's instructions to women from the minutes she had taken in Nauvoo. The minutes, Joseph had taught, were to be the society's "Constitution and law." Using this template for organizational structure and procedure, Eliza worked with women and their bishops to reestablish Relief Society on a permanent basis. Since its last recorded meeting in Nauvoo in March 1844, it had functioned only briefly

---

10. Spencer and Harmer, *Brigham Young at Home*, 76–77.
11. Snow, "Sketch," in Beecher, *Personal Writings*, 35.

OPPOSITE: *Eliza's lace bonnet, lace gloves, and blue silk purse. The gold watch was given to Eliza by Joseph Smith.*

in Utah from 1854 to 1858. Eliza's Nauvoo minute book became a model for women's record keeping. In some instances she even inaugurated the minute book for a particular ward by inscribing a title page patterned after the title page of her Nauvoo minutes or recording minutes of the first few meetings. She taught the importance of a good secretary and emphasized the essential role of the visiting committee, or teachers, known today as visiting teachers. She taught women in Provo, Utah, in 1869: "I say to my sisters who are called to be Teachers, when you visit, do all the good you can[;] if any such are cast down, who have lost the spirit of the Lord, speak words of encouragement to them, and impart of the spirit from your own bosom to enlighten and bring [them] back to the light of the gospel. We must act the part of the mother who when she sees her infant cold and chilly instead of pushing it from her, she seeks to resuscitate it by clasping it in her bosom, and imparting of her own warmth."[12]

Shortly after Brigham Young invited Eliza to work with bishops administratively, he "told [her] he was going to give [her] another mission." She was "'*to instruct the sisters.*'"[13] She soon expanded her long-honed writing skills into powerful speaking skills, using the pulpit more than the pen to elaborate and magnify the purposes of Relief Society as she traveled from ward to ward. She emphasized that although the women were to be largely self-governing, they must willingly accept counsel and direction from priesthood leaders. Most important, in terms of her assignment to instruct, she taught that Relief Society was to enliven women with a sense of their high and holy callings as daughters of God.[14] She addressed hundreds of women's gatherings, and many of her words are recorded in local minute books. For example, she spoke plainly to women in Lehi, Utah, in October 1869:

---

12. Provo Second Ward, Relief Society Minutes, 1869–1882, September 1869, manuscript, Church History Library; spelling standardized.
13. Snow, "Sketch," in Beecher, *Personal Writings,* 35.
14. See Jill Mulvay Derr, "Form and Feeling in a Carefully Crafted Life: Eliza R. Snow's 'Poem of Poems,'" *Journal of Mormon History* 26, no. 1 (Spring 2000): 21.

While sitting here I have been looking upon the faces of my sisters and can see the form of deity there and I have been reflecting on the great work we have to perform, even in helping in the salvation of the living and the dead. The Lord has organized these societies that we may gain knowledge and practice in an organized capacity and learn to respect our labors and one another and give honor where honor is due. We want to be ladies in very deed, not according to the term of the word as the world judges but fit companions of the gods and holy ones.

We have got to cooperate not only with our husbands but with God so that we may become saviors upon Mount Zion, for it is one thing to be a savior and another to be saved, one thing to be a queen and govern and control, and another to be a subject and be governed. Women should be women and not babies that need petting and correction all the time. I know we like to be appreciated but if we do not get all the appreciation which we think is our due, what matters? We know the Lord's laid high responsibility upon us, and there is not a wish or desire that the Lord has implanted in our hearts in righteousness but will be realized.[15]

At this Relief Society meeting, as at many others, Eliza expressed her support for the principle of plural marriage. Indeed, in the early months of 1870 she helped rally women in voicing their firm objections to anti-polygamy legislation pending in Congress. With impressive strength and certitude, Latter-day Saint women articulated their grievances, appealed for their rights and the rights of their husbands, fathers, and brothers, and supported plural marriage. Through the "indignation meetings," as they were known, Eliza and her sisters made a dramatic entry into public life. Their civic

---

15. Lehi Ward, Relief Society Minutes, vol. 1, 1868–1879, October 27, 1869, Church History Library; spelling and punctuation standardized.

*Elizabeth Ann Whitney (left), Emmeline B. Wells (center), and Eliza R. Snow (right)
advanced the work of Relief Society in the nineteenth century.
Photograph by Charles R. Savage, about 1876.*

activism increased after February 1870, when the territorial legislature passed an act enfranchising Utah women.

Eliza and the many women who traveled with her and labored as local Relief Society leaders witnessed the transformation Relief Society worked in the lives of those who participated. Eliza's close associate Emmeline B. Wells remarked in Manti, Utah, in 1884: "When contrasting how low spirited and weary the sisters were before the Relief Societies were organized, I think, What a blessing that we can meet and talk of the goodness of God and bear our testimonies to each other."[16]

Such changes were welcomed, and more organizational innovation followed. Throughout 1870, following another commission from Brigham Young, Eliza became engaged in promoting organizations for younger women. Originally known as Retrenchment Associations and later as Young Ladies' Mutual Improvement Associations, these new ward organizations provided younger women with opportunities for learning, speaking, and associating with such wise and experienced women as Eliza.

"Sister Eliza" provided central direction for the many achievements of Mormon women through the 1870s as they launched cooperative stores, engaged in home manufacture (including the manufacture of silk), produced their own newspaper, the *Woman's Exponent,* and began sending women to medical colleges. Zion's Poetess was becoming known as Zion's "Presidentess." In both capacities Eliza was often called upon to represent Latter-day Saint women. In August 1872, Brigham Young's secretary wrote a San Francisco woman inquiring about the Church: "If you wish to open up a correspondence on the subject, I would respectfully refer you to Miss Eliza R. Snow of S. L. City, a lady well versed in all matters pertaining to our religion; who is altogether competent to give you the desired information."[17]

---

16. Manti North Ward, Relief Society Minutes, 1883–1889, September 17, 1884, manuscript, Church History Library.

17. Letter from Brigham Young's secretary D[avid] McKenzie to Miss Helen H. Lindsey, August 21, 1872, Brigham Young Office Files transcription, Box 13, fd. 3, Church History Library.

Salt Lake City, about 1868.

Eliza frequently met with tourists and visitors to Utah, whose numbers increased dramatically after the completion of the transcontinental railroad in 1869. These were most often men and women of other faiths, some of whom took up residence in the territory. On more than one occasion, Eliza wrote a poem in honor of a "Gentile," that is, a non-Latter-day Saint. In one poem, although she did not identify the visitor, she sought to capture their conversation:[18]

<table>
<tr><td>

The Gentile's Queries

Lady, 'tis strange! How could you leave
    Your home, so lov'd—so dear—
Fond, loving hearts that hourly grieve;
    To dwell with Mormons here?

Why leave refinement's choicest courts,
    Where noblest feelings stir'd;
To mingle in the common sorts
    Of this low Mormon herd?

Why leave affection's cradled shrine
    Where kindness never tires—
Where gems of virtue brightly shine;
    To dwell in Mormon fires?

</td><td>

The Saint's Reply

Hush, stranger, hush: those words of gall
    Are not for me to hear:
Believe me, such expressions fall
    Like lava on my ear.

Tis true, I left fond hearts and dear
    A lov'd and beauteous home;
But I am blest in being here
    And wish my friends to come.

For here the richest fountain flows
    From heav'n's celestial sphere—
The highest boon that God bestows
    On man, is prosper'd here.

</td></tr>
</table>

---

18. This is the entire poem. Snow copied it into her journal, but it is undated and unpublished. See *Complete Poetry*, 789–90.

Eliza continued during this time to share her faith through her hymn writing. It is almost impossible to imagine Latter-day Saint hymnody without her three beloved sacrament hymns, all published in 1871: "Again We Meet around the Board," "Behold the Great Redeemer Die," and "How Great the Wisdom and the Love."[19] These profound and heartfelt texts pour forth Eliza's rich understanding of the Atonement. "How Great the Wisdom and the Love" is perhaps the most memorable of all. Eliza presented the fundamental truth of the Savior's sacrifice and the emblems of that sacrifice in a fresh and thoughtful way. The Savior's mission on earth was not a last-minute emergency measure but part of a plan that had been established long before the earth's creation. Eliza stepped back in time, back into the eternities, and began her poem with a scene placed in the distant reaches of time:

> How great the wisdom and the love
>   That fill'd the courts on high,
> And sent the Savior from above
>   To suffer, bleed and die!
>
> His precious blood He freely spilt—
>   His life He freely gave:
> A sinless sacrifice for guilt,
>   A dying world to save.
>
> Thro' strict obed'ence Jesus won
>   The prize with glory rife:
> "Thy will O God, not mine, be done,"
>   Adorn'd his mortal life.
>
> He mark'd the path and led the way,
>   And every point defines,

---

19. *Hymns* (1985), nos. 186, 191, and 195, respectively.

To light and life and endless day,
Where God's full presence shines.

How great, how glorious and complete,
Redemption's grand design;
Where justice, love and mercy meet
In harmony divine!

In mem'ry of the broken flesh
We eat the broken bread;
And witness with the cup, afresh,
Our faith in Christ, our head.[20]

Stanza 5 is used as the final verse in our hymnbook today. Perhaps no one has ever written a more elegant, reverent, and satisfying poetic summary of the gift of redemption, all in these four brief lines.

One of Eliza's finest poems is her testimony of the Savior's redemption of mankind. The poem, "A Winter Soliloquy," is written in the ten-syllable line known as iambic pentameter. It begins with a frightening description of winter's icy destruction. In nature, spring always follows winter, bringing forth blossoms from seeds lying dormant in the ground. But what about man? He, too, is laid in the ground when he dies, is a prisoner of death, doomed to "rise no more." But in a triumphant conclusion, the heavens open, and the Savior appears to "break the icy chain" of death and winter. Skillfully, with wonderful final lines, Eliza brought the poem full circle, paradoxically referring to the foreboding "winter" lines that opened the poem even as she proclaimed man's glorious immortality:

I hear—I see its tread as Winter comes—
Clad in white robes, how terribly august!
Its voice spreads terror—ev'ry step is mark'd

---

20. This text was first published in 1871. See *Complete Poetry*, 840–42.

With devastation! Nature in affright,
Languid and lifeless, sinks before the blast.

Should nature mourn? No: gentle Spring, ere long,
Will reascend the desolated throne:
Her animating voice will rouse from death,
Emerging from its chains, more beauteous far,
The world of variegated Nature.

Not so with man—Rais'd from the lowly dust,
He blooms awhile; but when he fades, he sets
To rise no more—on earth no more to bloom!
Swift is his course and sudden his decline!
Behold, to-day, his pulse beat high with hope—
His arms extended for the eager grasp
Of pleasure's phantom, fancy's golden ken
Paints in a gilded image on his heart.
Behold, to-morrow where? Ah! who can tell?
Ye slumb'ring tenants, will not you reply?
No: from his bow, death has a quiver sent,
And seal'd your senses in a torpid sleep.
Then who can tell? The living know him not:
Altho' perhaps, a friend or two, may drop
A tear, and say he's gone—she is no more!

Hark! from on high a glorious sound is heard,
Rife with rich music in eternal strains.
The op'ning heavens, by revelation's voice
Proclaim the key of knowledge unto man.

A Savior comes—He breaks the icy chain;
And man, resuscitated from the grave,
Awakes to life and immortality,

To be himself—more perfectly himself,

Than e'er he bloom'd in the primeval state

Of his existence in this wintry world.[21]

In February 1872, Eliza watched at the bedside of her beloved older sister, Leonora Snow Leavitt Morley, and saw "the last faint breath" that signaled her death and left Eliza "desolate" for a season. The poem she later composed in memory of her sister affirmed Eliza's belief in the awakening "to life and immortality" so eloquently described in "A Winter Soliloquy."[22]

In October 1872, Eliza embarked on the kind of expedition that even today most people can only dream of. It was the longest journey of her life, covering twenty-five thousand miles and lasting almost nine months. During that time, with her brother

Jerusalem, about 1872.

21. The entire text of this undated poem appears here. See *Complete Poetry*, 825–26.

22. Lines 19 and 24 of an 86-line poem in honor of Snow's sister, "My Sister, Leonora A. Morley." See *Complete Poetry*, 849–52.

Lorenzo and a small group of Church leaders she would visit London, Paris, Amsterdam, Florence, Rome, Venice, Vienna, Berlin, and many other cities. They would also travel to the Middle East, including Palestine, the Holy Land. Decades earlier, the Prophet Joseph had told her, *"You will yet visit Jerusalem,"* but the possibility of such a visit had seemed so unlikely that the "strange prediction had entirely gone from my memory," she wrote later, "even when invited to join the Tourist party, although the anticipation of standing on the sacredly celebrated Mount of Olives inspired me with a feeling no language can describe; Joseph Smith's prediction did not occur to me until within a very few days of the time set for starting, when a friend brought it to my recollection. . . . While on the tour, the knowledge of that prediction inspired

Photograph taken in Cairo, Egypt, in 1873 by H. Delie & E. Bechard before an exotic backdrop in their studio.

me with strength and fortitude." The travelers were, as Eliza said, a "Tourist party," sometimes called "the Palestine Tourists," but they were also an official Church delegation with the assignment to report on missionary work overseas and on the possibility of opening new missions. Most important, they were to dedicate the land of Palestine for the return of the Jews.[23]

The official head of the delegation was George A. Smith, first counselor to Brigham Young. Other travelers included Paul Augustus Schettler, a multilingual

---

23. Snow, "Sketch," in Beecher, *Personal Writings*, 38–39.

native of Prussia who served as the group's translator; Feramorz Little, a Salt Lake businessman (later elected mayor), and his eighteen-year-old daughter, Clara, who was Eliza's roommate for most of the trip; and other missionaries and Church leaders who joined them at various points on their extended journey. Elder Albert Carrington, a member of the Quorum of the Twelve Apostles then serving as president of the European Mission, joined them in Europe.

Eliza's travel was largely funded by donations of Latter-day Saint women through their ward Relief Societies. She wrote a poem thanking the women for their "beneficence unsought" and for "every kindness shown."[24] As a way of sharing her travels with these generous sisters, she wrote numerous letters and poems for publication in the Woman's Exponent. Her brother Lorenzo, George A. Smith, and Paul Schettler also wrote as they traveled. After her return, Eliza edited these writings as a 386-page book, *Correspondence of Palestine Tourists,* made up of selected letters, poems, and reminiscences, which was published by the Deseret News Press in 1875.

Eliza was sixty-eight years old when she left on the trip, the oldest of the group by ten years. She was a hardy traveler, however—Orson Whitney even noted upon her return the next year that she was "invigorated mentally and physically"[25]—and she handled the strains of travel wonderfully. In a letter to her mother, young Clara Little described a scene in their steamship cabin during the sea voyage to Liverpool:

"Aunt Eliza and I nearly wore out the carpet, sliding around. We were thrown out of our berths to the floor, and every time we attempted to stand, the ship would give a terrible lurch, and the waves would dash against it, and down we came; finally I got to the sofa and as soon as I could speak, I asked Aunt Eliza if she had found herself yet? She replied, 'Yes, but I am not able to find the bed.' So out I got, as bold as a lion, to try to help her, when, all of a sudden, she scaled by under the bed and went against the door. I . . . was bruised from head to foot, but was nearly dying to laugh. I imagine

---

24. "Responsive: To My Magnanimous Friends," published in *Woman's Exponent,* November 1, 1872. See *Complete Poetry,* 854–55.
25. Whitney, *History of Utah,* 4:575.

how comical we must have looked. Presently, she slides out from under the bed and we get right side up with care, and had a good laugh."[26] Eliza was not daunted by the roughness of the thirteen-day voyage. The first poem she wrote on the trip was called "Crossing the Atlantic." She speaks of "Neptune's furies" and the "tumbling, dashing" waves, but she knows that there is safety in "the God who made the waters."[27] Other poems followed, with titles that give an overview of the group's many experiences: "London," "Farewell to Paris," "Florence," "Sunrise on the Mediterranean," "On the Mount of Olives," "Apostrophe to Jerusalem," "At the Sea of Galilee."

On the Mount of Olives, the group dedicated Palestine for the gathering of the Jews.[28] Eliza called this the "crowning point" of the trip. A tent was prepared to offer privacy for the sacred ceremony. Eliza described the event for the *Woman's Exponent*:

"After an opening prayer by Brother Carrington, we united in service in the order of the Holy Priesthood, President Smith leading in humble, fervent supplication, dedicating the land of Palestine for the gathering of the Jews and the rebuilding of Jerusalem, and returning heartfelt thanks and gratitude to God for the fullness of the Gospel and the blessing bestowed on the Latter-day Saints. Other brethren led in turn, and we had a very interesting season; to me it seemed the crowning point of the whole tour, realizing as I did that we were worshipping on the summit of the sacred Mount, once the frequent resort of the Prince of Life."[29]

As she viewed such famous tourist attractions as Westminster Abbey, the Louvre Museum, Notre Dame Cathedral, and the canals of Venice, Eliza was constantly aware of her duty to represent the Church. Her perspective was not so much that of a poet as that of a Saint, and in her letters and poems she tended to scold the Europeans

---

26. Little, as quoted in Little, *Biographical Sketch*, 71.

27. Lines 24 and 57 of a 64-line poem titled "Crossing the Atlantic," published in *Woman's Exponent*, January 1, 1873, after it had arrived by mail. See *Complete Poetry*, 855–58.

28. On October 24, 1841, Orson Hyde of the Quorum of the Twelve Apostles recorded a prayer of dedication as he stood on the Mount of Olives.

29. Letter to the Editor of *Woman's Exponent*, March 9, 1873, published in George A. Smith et al., *Correspondence of Palestine Tourists*, 260.

for their materialism and for their lack of response to the gospel message. Perhaps for that reason, her travel poems are not among her best. When she returned to America and in much less dazzling surroundings, however, she wrote one of her most insightful and touching poems. On their return from the east coast, Eliza and her brother Lorenzo stopped in Ohio to visit their childhood home. Eliza had been absent for thirty-four years. They met with friends and relatives; Eliza reported that "even children born since we left that country came distances to see and converse with us, the former friends of their deceased parents. We visited night and day."[30] At such a reunion, the passing years inevitably manifest themselves on the faces of our loved ones, and we are compelled to realize that time and age have taken the same inexorable toll on us. Here is Eliza's wistful, honest poem:

> Our former, loved associates,
>   Have mostly passed away;
> While those we knew as children
>   Are crowned with locks of gray.
>
> We saw Time's varied traces,
>   Were deep on every hand—
> Indeed, upon the people,
>   More mark'd, than on the land.
>
> The hands that once, with firmness,
>   Could grasp the ax and blade,
> Now move with trembling motion,
>   By strength of nerve decay'd.
>
> The change in form and feature,
>   And furrows on the cheek;
> Of time's increasing volume,
>   In plain, round numbers speak,

---

30. Smith et al., *Correspondence of Palestine Tourists*, 381.

And thus, as in a mirror's
Reflection, we were told,
With stereotyp'd impressions,
The fact of growing old.[31]

Eliza had seen the vast world; she had visited the people of many other lands; and her response, when she returned, was to treasure even more the kingdom of God as it was being built by the Saints. She addressed the women of Zion one month after her return: "I thought when I was abroad, I thought before I went, and I have thought much since I returned, how necessary for the Saints of the living God to be more of a distinct people than what they are, to be the Saints of God in very deed—and to be as different from the world as our privileges are more exalted—we should be a shining light to the nations of the earth. . . . We are privileged above all other woman-kind."[32]

---

31. The letter addressed to the *Woman's Exponent* and containing this poem is dated June 20, 1873. It was published in the *Exponent* on August 1, 1873. See *Complete Poetry*, 879–80.

32. Snow, "An Address," *Woman's Exponent* 2 (September 15, 1873): 62.

St. George Looking North, *by Al Rounds. The St. George Temple, dedicated in 1877, was the first temple completed after the Saints' exodus from Nauvoo. The temple played a significant role in Eliza's visit to St. George in 1880–81.*

GOD WILL GIVE YOU GRACE TO STAND

1874–1887

Early in the evening of January 21, 1874, friends of Eliza R. Snow surprised her with a party marking her seventieth birthday. They praised her "richest rarest gifts" and expressed "gratitude / For all thy teachings and examples good."[1] More than ever, Eliza was a public figure, prominent both for her poetry and her dynamic and highly visible leadership of Latter-day Saint women.

At age seventy, with a lifetime of accomplishment and recognition already behind her, Eliza might have been expected to keep a less rigorous schedule. She had inspired Saints with her hymns and other poems; she was honored throughout Utah Territory as a leader and organizer; she had traveled to Europe and the Holy Land with an official delegation of the Church; for almost forty years she had faced hardship and triumph with her fellow Saints, and her words of faith, as well as her personal example, were known to Church members of all ages. Why not settle back and enjoy the tributes and honors that would come her way, the rewards of all her hard work? Why not ready a few more poems for *Poems 2* (published in 1877) and then live out some years of pleasant retirement with friends and family?

But it was not to be. As amazing as her many other accomplishments were,

---

1. "Birth-day Greeting," *Woman's Exponent* 2 (February 1, 1874): 132.

nothing in her life is more extraordinary than the spark of commitment and creativity that energized her final years. Though the events of these years were to tax Eliza to the utmost, emotionally and physically, the Lord continued to answer the prayer that she had written thirty years earlier in her diary: "O Lord my God I pray for health that I may be useful."[2] With unflagging determination, she devoted herself to the building of Zion—a pure, unified people—and she constantly testified to the prophetic calling of Joseph Smith and the truth of the restored gospel of Jesus Christ. More than ever she worked closely with Brigham Young and traveled widely to strengthen the women and youth of the Church. She continued her ministrations in the Endowment House and engaged in temple ordinance work in the newly completed temples at St. George to the south and Logan to the north. As she aged, she felt with particular gratitude the closeness of family and friends. With her often-affirmed belief that the Lord's covenant people would prevail in the end and be rewarded for their faithful endurance, Eliza had hoped to live to see a time of growth and peace in the valleys of the mountains. Yet a cloud of threat and uncertainty hung over these years. The federal government escalated its legislative and judicial campaign to end the Latter-day Saints' practice of plural marriage and to limit the Church's economic and political power. Eliza did not live to see the end of these painful conflicts, but she stood firm in the midst of them, encouraging others to "watch and pray, / And ever true and faithful be."[3]

Through the 1870s and 1880s, Utah Territory witnessed a steady increase of visitors and new residents of other faiths. The changing population and politics gradually eroded the autonomy and independence that Latter-day Saints had defined so clearly in their early years in the Great Basin. In Salt Lake City a new Catholic church was dedicated in 1871, an Episcopal cathedral was consecrated in 1874, and Methodists began holding camp meetings. Those of other faiths often vigorously opposed Latter-day Saint beliefs and practices, while Latter-day Saints considered Catholics and Protestants

2. Snow, Diary, June 24, 1846, in Beecher, *Personal Writings,* 137.
3. Lines 41 and 42 of "Evening Thoughts," a 44-line poem published in *Woman's Exponent,* September 1, 1887. See *Complete Poetry,* 1040–41.

to be "Gentiles" and discouraged members from patronizing their local businesses and schools or adopting their fashions. Eliza supported Church leaders' continuing campaign to maintain boundaries between the Latter-day Saint community and the outside world. "We don't know each other by our dress or looks from those in Babylon," she said in 1875. "We have got to lay off Babylon."[4] "Encourage HOME MANUFACTURE, it helps bring in the United Order," she told women in Ephraim, Utah.[5] She was supporting, as she so often did, Brigham Young's emphasis on establishing cooperative enterprises within individual communities, both to reinforce economic self-sufficiency and to strengthen unity. "Divide not your interest between heaven and earth nor copy worldly folly"[6] was counsel she often dispensed to young ladies in the ward Retrenchment Associations she deemed so important. She pushed young women to understand both their capacities and sacred responsibilities. On occasion, she dispensed similar counsel to young men. She reported to Relief Society women gathered in Salt Lake City in May 1875 that she had recently traveled southward to the town of Lehi, where she held a meeting for young ladies and invited them to bring their beaux: "I asked the young men to vote and told them I wanted them to sustain the young ladies in their positions; and also if they did not leave off their drinking and tobacco where were the young girls to get husbands? The young men did not wish the young girls to be in advance of them. I heard the next morning that the young men had been after the Bishop to organize them before night."[7] June 1875 marked the formal beginning of the Young Men's Mutual Improvement Association, under the direction of Brigham Young.

By 1875 Eliza was giving counsel and direction for virtually every program in

---

4. "A Short Synopsis of the Annual Meeting of the 19th Ward R. S., held at the Ward Hall, Aug. 18th," *Woman's Exponent* 4 (October 1, 1875): 67.

5. "Minutes of a Meeting Held at Ephraim, Sanpete Co., Friday, June 25th, 1875," *Woman's Exponent* 4 (August 15, 1875): 42–43.

6. Brigham City Relief Society Minutes, vol. 3, 1875–1884, September 10, 1878, manuscript, Church History Library, The Church of Jesus Christ of Latter-day Saints, Salt Lake City, Utah; hereafter cited as Church History Library.

7. Retrenchment Minutes, 1871–1875, May 1, 1875, Church History Library.

WOMAN'S EXPONENT.

VOL. 6.   SALT LAKE CITY, UTAH, AUGUST 15, 1877.   No. 6.

[For the EXPONENT.]

THOUGHTS AND MEMORIES OF A SUMMER HOUR.

Mem'ry is busy in her haunted bow'r,
  Clad with bright thoughts the senses to beguile;
So softly falls the touch of passing hour,
  That dreamy fancies linger near the while.

I hear soft voices murmur'ng low and sweet;
  I feel the touch of gentle hands again;
And in the shadow of some lone retreat,
  I e'en forgot I ever suffer'd pain.

Tears fall and mingle with the pearly dew,
  And flow'rs spring up afresh where all was drear;
And something whispers of a life more true,
  Where perfect love will reign, devoid of fear.

There seems a rapture in the summer breeze,
  Borne from some region ever bright and fair;
How lovingly it plays amid the trees,
  Breathing "enchantment in the azure air."

O memory of the years now past away,
  Buried and dead, but living still in thought;
Nature was then as prescient as to-day,
  And her conceptions were as grandly wrought.

Earth rob'd herself as queenly then, as now,
  And summer mantled hill, and field, and plain,
And garlanded with flow'rs her blushing brow,
  And wreath'd her sceptre with the golden grain.

Yes, other summers have in glory woke,
  And sunshine flooded nature with its kiss;
But time's relentless hand the spell has broke,
  Though earth were in an ecstacy of bliss.

In the weird rustle of the falling leaves,
  There is a sadness touching to the heart,
For summer her departing glory grieves,
  Yet nobly doth she with her treasures part.

She sighs her requiem to the passing breeze;
  All nature joins her in the mournful strain;
A thousand echoes whisper in the trees,
  Repeating o'er and o'er the sad refrain.

And is there in our hearts no sad regret,
  No mem'ries of the last year's falling leaves?
Shall we the sweetness of the past forget?
  Or glean, and garner it in mem'ry's sheaves,

Where fancy's magic wand can recreate,
  And live again the happy seasons o'er,
Food for the mind, 'gainst bitter, adverse fate,
  Harvest of thoughts to gladden evermore.

Salt Lake City, August 11, 1877.   EMILE.

PSALM: FOR THE TWENTY-FOURTH OF JULY, 1877.

WRITTEN FOR MASTER ANDERSON, BY E. R. SNOW.

In all our assemblies we will chant the praises of the Lord God of Hosts.

His spirit is the soul of our entertainments—the interest of His kingdom the incentive of all our efforts.

God, who inhabits eternity—who dwells in the fulness of light—who speaks and all the Intelligences in the courts on high give audience:

He is the God of Abraham, Isaac, Jacob, Joseph, Brigham, and of all true Latterday Saints.

Blessed are those that trust in Him—who obey the voice of His servants—who rejoice in the purity of His ordinances, and the justice and equity of His statutes.

He sent the angel Moroni to announce to Joseph the introduction of the Dispensation of the fulness of times: He sent Peter, James and John to commit to him the keys of the Kingdom of heaven.

Through Joseph, He revealed the principles of righteousness, and laid the foundation of a government of peace.

Though small in the beginning, and a theme of derision among the scribes and pharisees of modern times, it is truly "a marvelous work and a wonder:" It has spread from nation to nation, and is now arousing the attention of the high ones of the earth.

It is gathering the honest in heart from every clime—the spirit of God is in their hearts, and the strong cords of faith and obedience draw them together.

They come, not laden with the gold of Ophir—they come not decked with the glittering ornaments and splendid attire of worldly grandeur; but through the tender mercies of Him who "tempers the storm to the shorn lamb," although destitute of Mammon's treasures, they come richly supplied with the more requisite capital for strengthening the stakes of Zion, and building the Temples of our God, even the brain, the bone and the sinew.

Through the blessings of the Most High on the labors of the husbandman, the parched and sterile soil has become productive and yields an abundance of the richest products.

The products of Utah are abundantly laden with material for the finest and richest fabrics; the most skillful artisans are here; and only united effort is wanting to ensure permanent success; and, ere long, the faithful in Zion will be clothed in garments more beautiful than those of earthly princes, and "the beauty thereof will be the work of their own hands."

Let us all, old and young—parents and children, take hold with our might, for the time has come when those who profess to be saints, must be saints in very deed.

There is a furnace in Zion—the fire thereof has already commenced to burn, and the heat will increase until iniquity shall be cleansed from our midst.

Then will the treasures of the earth, the treasures of the deep, and the treasures of the heavens above, be poured out in great abundance.

Then will the beauty of Zion shine forth clear as the sun at noonday: She will arise terrible in might—the glory of God will fill her courts, and celestial beings will minister in her holy places.

Glory, honor, praise and adoration be unto our God.

WOMAN'S RECORD.

MISS ROSE HALL, of Middlesex, England, has allowed her goods to be distrained for Queen's taxes, as a practical protest against the exclusion of women householders from the Parliamentary franchise. Twelve silver forks were seized and put up at auction.

MRS. M. B. C. SLADE is to be the editor of a new monthly magazine, entitled "Good Times," which will be issued August 1st, devoted to entertaining, amusing and instructive dialogues, recitations, declamations, and selections; tableaux; motion-songs, and other musical varieties, for exhibitions and public exercises.

MISS BETTIE VAN LEW occasioned a slight flutter in the office of the City Collector, day before yesterday, says the Richmond, (Va.) "Enquirer." Her appearance there was perhaps explained by the following indorsement on a paper which she passed over to the Collector, inclosing $200, the amount of her tax bill: "Richmond, June 29.—Taxes paid under protest, having bitterly realized the need of the ballot, and being, as a woman, denied that right.—Elizabeth L. Van Lew." This Miss Bettie Van Lew is the plucky Republican postmistress of Richmond, Va., lately displaced by President Hayes.—Ex.

NOTES AND NEWS.

DR. SCHLIEMANN; the celebrated explorer of Trojan and Greek mines, is expected to visit America.

AN EXPEDITION, consisting of Lieut. Wood, U. S. Army, and Prof. Taylor of the University of Chicago, with some assistants, has gone to Alaska, to ascertain the height of Mt. Elias.

A STATUE of King Alfred the Great was unveiled at Wantage, England, on Saturday, July 31st, by the Prince of Wales. It is sculptured in marble, and was executed by Count Gleichen, the queen's cousin, at a cost of about $10,000. Wantage is the place where King Alfred was born.

IT SEEMS to be conceded, that among the members of Parliament most likely to become future Premiers of the British government, is Mr. Chamberlain who, having accumulated a fortune in manufactures, is now devoting his fine abilities to public affairs. Just now the most rising member of the House of Commons is Mr. Leonard Courtney, one of the ablest and most scholarly of the leader-writers on the London "Times." Both Mr. Chamberlain and Mr. Courtney have distinguished themselves by their advocacy of the Woman Suffrage Bill, which seems to be rapidly gaining strength in England.—Ex.

The laboratories for women at the Institute of Technology are well worth the attention of those who are interested in the higher education of women. They were established about six months ago, at the request and with the assistance of the Woman's Education Association, and are designed "to afford facilities for the advanced study of Chemical Analysis, Mineralogy, and Chemistry, as related to Vegetable and Animal Physiology and to the Industrial Arts." Any subject may be studied separately; there are no classes, each pupil working by herself under the immediate and practical instruction of Prof. John M. Ordway or of Mrs. Richards. The microscopic work, and physiological chemistry, seem especially adapted to women, and offer honorable employment to those who are skilled.—"Boston Correspondent Worcester Spy."

Salt Lake City's Old Constitution Building.

which Mormon women were engaged at the ward level: home industry, silk cultivation, obstetrical training, and grain storage—all featured in the pages of their semimonthly newspaper, the *Woman's Exponent*. Late that year, in a departure from her characteristic isolationism, she agreed to oversee Utah women's participation in the national bicentennial exhibition planned for Philadelphia. "I selected and organized a Committee of twelve, composed of 'Mormon' and Gentile Ladies—got up a printed Circular which we sent post-haste to all Presidents of Relief Societies, and Young Ladies Associations, calling for a united Co-operation in preparing and collecting specimens that should be worthy our representation, and do honor to our grand National Centennial Fair."[8] The "specimens" of women's handiwork came in, but the territorial legislature funded shipping for only a small number of "choice, light articles,"[9] so the rest were featured at a "Territorial Fair" held, appropriately, in Salt Lake City's Constitution Building through the summer of 1876. As the fair closed, President Young recommended that the women extend their efforts to feature their handmade goods. In the same building, women launched a new enterprise,

8. Snow, "Sketch," in Beecher, *Personal Writings*, 37–38.
9. Snow, "Sketch," in Beecher, *Personal Writings*, 38.

the Woman's Commission House or cooperative store. In 1877, among the hand-work featured in the store, was a blue banner with a motto embroidered in white: "In Union Is Strength,"[10] Whether or not it was the work of accomplished seamstress and short-term store manager Eliza Snow, it was a sentiment she often expressed. She was an integral part of the efforts that intensified the Saints' sense of community and identity.

The death in 1877 of Brigham Young, her husband of thirty-three years whom she called "the master spirit of the age," marked the end of the life Eliza had known within the family and within the Church organization. She arranged for volume 2 of *Poems: Religious, Political, and Historical* to begin and end with poems in his honor; the already-composed opening poem dedicated the volume to him, and the final poem ended with her funeral tribute. She painted an elegant, detailed picture of the funeral of Brigham Young:

> *Decked with pure white flowers,*
> *Hallow'd with tear-drops from the eyes of those*
> *Whose skilful hands, prompted by loving hearts,*
> *In wreaths entwined them; there the coffin stood, . . .*
> *And mourning sat on every countenance,*
> *As though the lights of earth had all gone out,*
> *And left a calm—an all pervading calm.*

At the funeral, Eliza tells us, Brigham's friends and coworkers—"men of God . . . whose hearts had never quailed"—were near to tears. But the mourners were comforted by thoughts of the power of God bestowed upon the leaders of his Church, past and future:

---

10. See Derr, Cannon, and Beecher, *Women of Covenant,* 83.

OPPOSITE: *Both "Anthem" and "Dedication" are poems composed in honor of Brigham Young* (Complete Poems, *632, 772). After "Dedication" appeared in the* Deseret News *in 1868, Eliza published it as the first poem in* Poems 2 *(also shown).*

> They knew the work that Brigham Young, so long,
>
> With master mind and skill had pioneered,
>
> Was God's—that He, his servants, heretofore,
>
> Had clothed with power and wisdom, and He now
>
> Would others clothe upon, and bear them off
>
> Triumphantly.[11]

As she planned her second volume of collected poems, Eliza polished new poems and also chose some of her previous work for inclusion. *Poems: Religious, Historical and Political, Volume 2,* was published in Salt Lake City in 1877. The subtitle *Religious, Historical, and Political* was the same description she had chosen for her 1856 volume, reminding her readers that she was not just a writer of hymns and celebratory poems. Her poems covered a great range of topics, as can be seen in some of the titles from *Poems 2:* "Immortality," "The Hopes of Heaven," "My Country—A Lamentation," "To Brigham Young," "The Lamanite," "Hints at Matters of Fact in Utah," "The Hypocrite and the Traitor," "Temple Song," and many others.

Volume 2 also contained a surprise—Eliza's longest poem, almost two thousand lines. She left no mention of this poem in the correspondence and other writings that remain to us, but she had probably been working on it for years, perhaps decades. Admittedly, the title is not very inviting: "Personification of Truth, Error, Etc.: An Epic Poem in Five Chapters."[12] But in many ways, "Personification" shows Eliza at her best. She used her favorite blank verse line form but interspersed it with shorter sections in other meters, and the story she tells is often witty and surprising, full of symbolism and imagination. With wonderful dramatic flair, she assigned dialogue and action to the various characters, who are "personifications" of human traits. In the first chapter, she painted an idyllic family scene, but the names of the family members—the mother is named Ignorance, the father is Prejudice, and their new baby is

---

11. Lines 19–22, 28-30, 31, 34, and 44–49 of "Funeral of President Brigham Young," a 96-line poem first published in *Poems* (1877). See *Complete Poetry,* 899–903.

12. *Complete Poetry,* 903–58.

Error—are a clue that something serious is about to happen. Ignorance worries that her baby is not thriving as he should. She secretly visits an advisor, named Suspicion, who warns Ignorance that she and her husband Prejudice must act quickly, because a rival youngster, Truth, is growing up in a neighboring land, and Truth hopes to conquer the kingdom that Error is expected to rule one day. So Ignorance and Prejudice come up with a plan: they decide to fake their own funerals so that Error can take charge of their kingdom before Truth has a chance to enter the scene.

Of course, Truth at last triumphs. In the meantime, characters enter the scene with such names as Pride, Envy, Avarice, Hate, Jealousy, Deceit, Fashion, and Stupidity. One of the funniest moments of the entire poem is the lullaby sung to Stupidity by his loving wife, whose name is Content. How Eliza must have smiled when she wrote these words of tender devotion in praise of Stupidity!

Error has a charm to bless—
Error's presence we possess;
Dearer far, than Happiness
    Is Stupidity.

Get you hence—ye works of Art,
With the treasures you impart—
Let me press me to the heart
    Of Stupidity.

Let Refinement come not here—
Nor Intelligence draw near
To the sphere—the blessed sphere
    Of Stupidity.

He is faithful to his trust—
Books may moulder—tools may rust—
All improvements lick the dust,
    With Stupidity.

O Stupidity, my Love:
Thou art gentle as the dove—
None but Error ranks above
Thee, Stupidity.[13]

In the summer of 1878, Eliza became engaged in her last major organizational innovation, implemented with the full support of John Taylor, president of the Quorum of the Twelve Apostles and the presiding officer of the Church after the death of Brigham Young. It is easy enough to imagine the following unremarkable scene: three friends are on a railway platform, waiting to board a train, and they pass the time in conversation. If, however, those friends are Eliza R. Snow, Emmeline B. Wells, and Aurelia S. Rogers, the combination of their inspired initiative is enough to result in worldwide impact. And how rapidly the three of them move to make their plans, enlist priesthood cooperation, and begin organizing! Eliza tells the story of the beginnings of the Primary Association:

"In August 1878, Mrs. Emmeline B. Wells and I, after attending a Conference of the Young Ladies in Farmington, Davis Co., spent an hour, waiting for the train, with Mrs. Aurelia Rogers. During our conversation, Mrs. R. expressed a desire that something more could be effected for the cultivation and improvement of the children morally and spiritually than was being done through the influence of day and Sunday-Schools. After consulting together a few moments, I asked Mrs. R. if she was willing to take the responsibility and labor on herself of presiding over the children of that settlement, provided the Bishop of the Ward sanctioned the movement. She replied in the affirmative. The train was near, and no time to consult the Bishop; but directly after arriving home, I wrote the Bishop, and by return Mail received from him a very satisfactory response, in which he, (Bishop Hess) not only gave his permission but hearty approval accompanied with his blessing. I then informed Mrs. Rogers that

---

13. Lines 305–8 and 321–36 of the second chapter of "Personification of Truth, Error, Etc.," published in *Poems* (1877). See *Complete Poetry*, 950–51.

she might consider herself authorized to proceed, and organize in Farmington, which she did, and I commenced in the eleventh Ward in Salt Lake City. We adopted the appellation of Primary Associations, and admit as members boys and girls from four to twelve, and in some instances, sixteen years of age."[14]

Thereafter, in company with other leading sisters, Eliza traveled widely to organize Primary Associations in each ward. Because she was committed to helping children "understand the principles of the Gospel" and "have its spirit in their hearts,"[15] she produced the Primary's first curriculum. She wrote a few new poems and recitations but largely drew from her earlier work and the work of others to compile and publish five books: *Children's Primary Hymn Book* (1880), *Children's Primary Tune Book* (1880), *Primary Speaker Book One* (1882), *Primary Speaker Book Two* (1882), and *Bible Questions and Answers* (1883).

Latter-day Saint children were growing up in a solicitous but embattled community. In 1879 the United States Supreme Court ruled that the practice of plural marriage was not protected under the First Amendment of the United States Constitution, as the Saints had long maintained. The 1882 Edmunds Act barred those living in plural marriage from jury service, public office, and voting. The 1887 Edmunds-Tucker Act, among other measures, disincorporated the Church and withdrew female suffrage in Utah Territory. As indictment and prosecution of Latter-day Saints for "cohabitation" steadily increased, many went to prison or into hiding, fracturing Mormon family life. Many families were affected, including the Snows; at the close of 1885, Eliza's brother Lorenzo was tried and then imprisoned for nearly a year, and Church president John Taylor was in exile when he died in July 1887. In these dangerous times, Snow decried the "base, lascivious heartless tools" seeking to "invade the pure domestic shrine" and "sever bonds divine."[16]

---

14. Snow, "Sketch," in Beecher, *Personal Writings*, 36–37.

15. "Report of the meeting held in Mt. Pleasant, Sanpete Co., August 7, 1880," *Woman's Exponent* 9 (October 1, 1880): 71.

16. Lines 14–16 of "Requiem," a 42-line poem published in *Deseret News*, July 9, 1885. See *Complete Poetry*, 1017–19.

In a prose poem composed in 1879, Eliza wrote these bitingly ironic words, lashing out at the federal officials who dared to interfere in Mormon life:

> *Yea, let us cause thousands of honorable, loving wives to be stigmatized as prostitutes, and their offspring as bastards.*

> *Let us cause multitudes of innocent children, that now are being tenderly cherished and educated, to be branded with infamy and deprived of heirship.*

> *Let us immure in loathsome prisons those brave men, who, for the sake of worshipping God according to the dictates of their consciences, left their homes and the graves of their noble ancestors, and sought refuge in the sterile American Desert.*[17]

In the wake of the legal decision that facilitated prosecution of those practicing plural marriage, Eliza became more adamant in her defense of the marriage ties that had defined the last half of her life. Beginning in 1880, after the deaths of Brigham Young (1877) and Emma Smith (1879), Eliza decided thereafter to be known as Eliza R. Snow Smith, thus openly declaring the reality of the principle of plural marriage and her testimony of the inspired leadership of Joseph Smith. She had defended plural marriage and acknowledged her relationship to Joseph Smith on many previous occasions, but changing her name was like hoisting a banner in a time of crisis. The Saints had publicly acknowledged the practice of plurality of wives in 1852.[18] When Joseph Smith III, eldest son of the Prophet, declared that his father "never could have promulgated such doctrines"[19] and when Emma Smith declared that her husband had never married plural wives nor sanctioned polygamy,[20] Eliza spoke out: Joseph

---

17. "Decision," a prose poem of 14 paragraphs, was published in *Deseret News,* January 21, 1879. See *Complete Poetry,* 967–69.
18. See Ludlow, *Encyclopedia of Mormonism,* 3:1091.
19. *Saints' Herald* 1 (May 1860): 101–5.
20. "Last Testimony of Sister Emma," *Saints' Herald* [Plano, Illinois] 26, no. 19 (October 1, 1879).

Smith III "better had waited until his father's wives were silent in death, for now they are living witnesses of the divinity of plural marriage, as revealed by the Almighty."[21]

Eliza's decision to be known as Eliza R. Snow Smith, thus identifying herself unmistakably as the wife of the Prophet Joseph, was significant during her remarkable five-month sojourn in southern Utah during the winter of 1880–81. Eliza did not hesitate to travel to wherever she was needed on behalf of the Young Women, the Primary, and especially the Relief Society. She proudly recalled, "I have traveled from one end of Utah Ter. to the other—into Nevada & Idaho, in the interests of these organizations—have organized hundreds of Young Ladies' and Primary Associations since their introduction."[22] The journey to St. George and the surrounding area was her last major trip, and it was not an easy one. She afterwards recalled "having traveled one thousand miles by team over jolting rocks and through bedded sand, occasionally camping out at night on long drives."[23]

Accompanying Eliza was her good friend Zina D. H. Young, who was also her first counselor in the newly organized general presidency of the Relief Society. After directing Relief Society programs for nearly twelve years, Eliza had been set apart as general president in July 1880.[24] A November article in the *Deseret News* had announced "Sister Eliza R. Snow and Zina D. Young are contemplating a trip to St. George, before winter sets in. They will start within the next fortnight probably, and return in about a month afterward."[25] In fact, they left just five days later and did not return for five months.[26]

---

21. Eliza R. Snow to Editors, *Deseret News,* October 18, 1879, 2.

22. Snow, "Sketch," in Beecher, *Personal Writings,* 37.

23. Snow, "Sketch," in Beecher, *Personal Writings,* 37.

24. The June 19, 1880, nomination and sustaining of Eliza R. Snow as "president of all the Relief Societies" is recorded in "Salt Lake Stake Relief Society Conference," *Woman's Exponent* 8 (July 1, 1880): 21–22. The setting apart of the Relief Society central board or general presidency nearly a month later is recorded in "Minutes of a General Meeting Held in Fourteenth Ward Assembly Hall, July 17th, 1880," under "Relief Society Reports," *Woman's Exponent* 9 (September 1, 1880): 53. The importance of both meetings is discussed in Derr, Cannon, and Beecher, *Women of Covenant,* 121–22.

25. "Going South," *Deseret News,* November 3, 1880, 625.

26. Derr, *Mrs. Smith Goes to Washington.*

The St. George Temple, under construction here, was dedicated in 1877.

What seems to have been originally planned as a visit to St. George, the temple, and members of the Young family and numerous friends expanded to include visits to nearly every settlement in five Utah counties: Millard, Beaver, Iron, Washington, and Kane. Between November 1880 and March 1881, Eliza and Zina circled through a series of thirty-two settlements and visited Relief Societies, Young Ladies organizations, and Primary Associations. Often the women held two meetings a day. The southern Saints welcomed Eliza at the crowning point of her influence, a moment when all facets of her personal and public presence came together. Elizabeth Little of Kanab wrote a tribute, published in the *Woman's Exponent:* "The bright halo of their great and noble souls will float around us," she predicted, "like the glory of the departed day or the gentle breeze of a Summer evening."[27]

---

27. "A Welcome," *Woman's Exponent* 9 (April 1, 1881): 165.

During this time in St. George, Eliza frequently spent time in the St. George Temple, performing proxy ordinances for her ancestors. Eliza's first temple work was to complete the saving ordinances for all female members of her immediate family, including her mother, Rosetta Pettibone Snow, and her sisters, Percy Amanda Snow McConoughey and Melissa Snow. For five weeks thereafter, Eliza and Zina spent nearly every Wednesday, Thursday, and Friday in temple service. Because they traveled so extensively, their schedule was less regular after that, but they spent a total of thirty-nine days in the St. George Temple, more than a quarter of their time in the south.

The St. George Temple was the first completed by the Saints after their 1846 exodus from Nauvoo. (Cornerstones for the Salt Lake Temple were laid in April 1853, but it was not completed and dedicated until 1893.) Parts of the St. George Temple were dedicated for use on January 1, 1877, and the remainder of the temple on April 6 of that year. Eliza wrote an anthem that was sung at the second dedication, though she did not attend.

> *Hark, hark! angelic minstrels sing*
> *A sweet, melodious strain;*
> *Heav'n's high, celestial arches ring*
> *With joyful news again.*
> *Lo! now another key is turned:*
> *'Tis God's divine behest;*
> *And those for whom our hearts have yearn'd,*
> *Our dead, again are blest.*
>
> *CHORUS.*
>
> *From the valleys of Ephraim hosannas arise,*
> *And new hallelujahs descend from the skies,*

Glad shouts of redemption from bondage resound
From the shades where the spirits in prison are bound.[28]

Like Eliza, Zina D. H. Young had been a plural wife first of Joseph Smith and, after Joseph's death, of Brigham Young. During their southern tour, the women celebrated their connection to Joseph and were honored as "wives of the Prophet Joseph Smith," even by Primary children. Eliza told the children in the town of Washington "that if anybody said that Joseph Smith never had but one wife to tell them that they knew better for they saw two of them at once namely Eliza R. Snow and Zina D. Young."[29] A decade after this tour, in 1890, the Church officially abandoned the practice of plural marriage, and it is not practiced in the Church today. Eliza died before this change was made, but had she lived, undoubtedly she would have found a way to support the new direction, as Zina did.

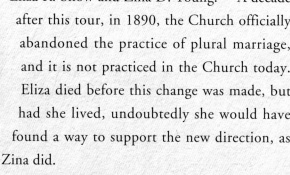

Zina D. H. Young.

Eliza and Zina organized more than thirty Primaries during their trip south. To help the children feel that they were part of the Primary organization from the outset, Eliza often asked the assembled children whether they wanted to be organized, teaching them, as she did in the town of Virgin, that "this was to be their own meeting." She asked the children in Pine Valley, "Who was the first prophet in the church? And who appeared to Joseph Smith?"[30] She told them about

28. Lines 1–12 of "Temple Song," a 36-line poem published in *Woman's Exponent*, February 15, 1877, and in *Juvenile Instructor* of the same date. See *Complete Poetry*, 895–96.
29. Washington Ward, St. George Stake, Primary Minutes, 1880–1887, November 19, 1880, Church History Library.
30. Virgin City Ward, St. George Stake, Primary Minutes, January 6, 1881, Church History Library.
OPPOSITE: *Eliza's lace, embroidered on fine white cotton. Photo of Eliza about 1868, by Edward Martin.*

TEMPLE SONG.

DS BY E. R. SNOW.

Moderato:

MUSIC BY PROF. C. J. THOMAS.

Hark, hark, an-gel-ic min-strels sing, A sweet mel-odi-ous train: Heav'n's

s ring With joy-ful news a - gain, Lo! now an-other key is turn'd; 'Tis God's di-vine be-hest,

CHORUS: *Allegretto*

ts have yearn'd, Our dead, a-gain are blessed. From the val-leys of Eph-ra'm ho-

w hal - le - lu - jahs de-scend from the skies, Glad shouts of re-demp-tion from

From the shades where the spir - its in pris - on are bound.

n baptized for them, and now,
nts in their stead,
shed and we're anointed too—
ving for the dead.

Within a Temple's sacred court—
  Beneath its royal tower,
Let humble, faithful Saints resort
  To wield salvation's power.
Salvation's work! O, glorious theme,
  Too high for mortal tongues;
Seraphic hosts its grace proclaim
  In everlasting songs.

Of great, momentous times at hand,
  Portending signs appear:
The wise will see and understand
  The day of God is near.
Ye heavenly gates, no more ajar—
  Henceforth stand open wide;
The Bridegroom's voice is heard afar,
  Prepare, prepare the Bride.

the Prophet Joseph and showed them the gold watch he had given her—a ritual she performed in nearly every Primary Association she visited. One woman from Cedar City recalled Eliza's meeting with the children:

"One of the most unforgettable things of my life was when Eliza R. Snow came to Cedar City in 1880 to organize a Primary Association. I was about six, and there were perhaps twenty of us who were charter members of that Primary.

"During the organization meeting Sister Snow showed us a watch which had been the Prophet Joseph's. She told us about the Prophet and the watch. She let each of us hold the watch for a short time. I remember as I held the watch in my tiny cupped hands, she gave us an admonition not to ever forget that we had held the Prophet's watch."[31]

One of Eliza's great strengths as a leader was her capacity to encourage and to elevate, to spark in women of all ages a sense of their own worth and divinity. Zina and Eliza met with Young Women as well. "The Young Ladies of Zion are greater than the Queens of the earth," she proclaimed in Santa Clara. "I would say to my young sisters, never shrink from a duty. God has put the means in your hands to become queens and priestesses, if you will only live for it."[32] "We are all Sisters and each of us have our parts to perform," Eliza told the women at Rockville as she organized a Relief Society there. "Be alive."[33]

On the afternoon of December 23, 1880, a commemoration was held in the social hall in St. George to mark the birthday of Joseph Smith. As Joseph's widows, Eliza and Zina were honored guests. Many people, including Eliza and Zina, shared early reminiscences of the Prophet, and as the celebration continued into the evening Susa

---

31. The gold watch is discussed in detail in Jennifer Reeder, "Eliza R. Snow and the Prophet's Gold Watch: Time Keeper as Relic," *Journal of Mormon History* 31, no. 1 (Spring 2005): 119–41. This reminiscence, from Violet Lunt Urie, is quoted on 137–38 of that article.

32. Santa Clara Ward, Relief Society Minutes, November 27, 1880, and December 28, 1880, Church History Library.

33. Rockville Ward Relief Society Minutes and Records, 4 January 1881, Church History Library.

Young Gates read a poem that Eliza had composed for the occasion. She praised his unique gifts and emphasized the restoration of priesthood and temple ordinances:

> *Harmoniously in him, at once combined*
> *Goodness of heart and strength of mastermind,*
> *Embodying childlike, sweet simplicity*
> *With superhuman, Godlike majesty,*

The temple, she wrote, "testifies / That Joseph Smith, the great, and good, and wise, / Is GOD's TRUE PROPHET."[34]

Zina's brother Oliver recorded that "at the close of their speeches, they both withdrew, and while they were withdrawing the whole audience rose upon their feet and stood, in honor of the wives of the Prophet Joseph Smith, the Prophet whose birth they had met to commemorate."[35] Eliza was moved: "It is almost worse than nothing for me to attempt to describe the touching ceremonies," she noted; "the time *never can be forgotten*."[36]

Following her immensely productive and significant trip to southern Utah, Eliza remained at the center of much of Latter-day Saint women's work. Boosting the cultivation of silk, speaking at young women's conferences, attending Primary fairs, chairing the board of the Relief Society's Deseret Hospital, personally presenting First Lady Lucy Hayes with a volume of her poems, Eliza's days were "crowded with labors."[37] In 1884, an English traveler to Salt Lake City met Eliza R. Snow and commented on her remarkable "vigor and enthusiasm."[38] At eighty years of age, Eliza was still greeting visitors, officiating in temple ordinances, preaching throughout the Territory of

---

34. Lines 23–26 and 67–69 of "Tribute to the Birthday of the Prophet Joseph," a 74-line poem published in *Deseret News,* February 2, 1881. See *Complete Poetry,* 976–79.

35. Diary of Oliver B. Huntington, 1847–1900, Part 2, December 23, 1880, Church History Library.

36. "Anniversary Party in St. George," *Woman's Exponent* 9 (January 1, 1881): 116–17.

37. Editor [George Q. Cannon], "Anniversary of Sister Eliza R. Snow Smith's Birth-day," *Juvenile Instructor,* February 1, 1884, 38.

38. Faithfull, *Three Visits to America,* 152, 180.

Utah, and writing. "Sister Eliza" remained "the recognized leader of the women of the Latter-day Saints."[39] Women's responsibilities in the Church would change somewhat over time, but the Relief Society, Young Women, and Primary would endure; Eliza and her sisters had created a lasting place for women in the structure of the Church.

As a woman in her eighties, Eliza wrote poems for friends and family and continued to employ her poetry as a medium for political protest. She remained remarkably in touch with the world around her and with her friends both young and old. She wrote many letters, both official and personal, and usually some combination of both since her network of friendships was so widespread. Her poems reflect her attachments to people and her concern for their temporal and spiritual well-being. In 1884, she wrote a poem called "Bridal Tribute." The couple for whom she wrote this poem will probably remain unknown—it is "Respectfully Inscribed to—They Know Whom"— but Eliza tenderly congratulated them on their worthiness to enter the temple and make eternal covenants:

> We wish you all the happiness
> > That in a wedded life can be
> Obtained through constant faithfulness
> > For time and all eternity.
>
> Within a Temple's sacred shrine,
> > When knelt beside an altar there,
> By rite performed as God enjoins,
> > You two became a wedded pair.
>
> Commenced aright:—now step by step
> > The upward leading track pursue;

---

39. [Emmeline B. Wells,] "Pen Sketch of an Illustrious Woman: Eliza R. Snow Smith," *Woman's Exponent* 10 (July 15, 1881): 27.

OPPOSITE: *A portrait of Lorenzo Snow, n.d., by Charles W. Carter; a letter (with envelope) written to Zina D. H. Young; and Eliza's gold mantle clock.*

Salt Lake City, May 10, 1886,

Zina D. H. Young,
My very Dear Sister,
Your kind letter
duly received and highly appreciated.
thanks for your motherly and
interest in my behalf. Sister Thomas
as regularly as the morning does
what we require.

Mrs. Zina D. H. Young,
Logan City,
Cache Co.,
Utah

> *Should obstacles arise, look up*
> *And keep the royal end in view.*
>
> *And now our blessing we extend*
> *In wishing you the rich behest*
> *That noble deeds and efforts bring,*
> *And say, "In blessing be you blest."*[40]

Eliza treasured Snow family ties with particular intensity and spent many days among Lorenzo's family in Brigham City. She undertook a major family history project, a 581-page *Biography and Family Record of Lorenzo Snow,* published in 1884. This work pays tribute to Lorenzo and his large family and captures some of Eliza's own life and poems as well.

In January 1884, Lorenzo Snow sent word to all his family—his descendants numbered "considerably over one hundred," he said—announcing a family reunion. He noted that "the seventieth anniversary of my birth" seemed "a suitable time" for the event. At the end of the three-day celebration, which consisted of dancing, speeches, recitations, and music, including a song written by Eliza in her brother's honor, Lorenzo offered a closing address in which he observed that the gathering was "the last family re-union we have reason to expect on this side of the spirit world."[41] Yet he lived another seventeen years and became the fifth president of the Church in 1898. Here is part of Eliza's song, titled "Our Father's Birthday":

> *Long may you live our lives to bless,*
> *And our young steps to guide,*
> *Until with Zion's righteousness,*
> *Your soul is satisfied—*

---

40. Lines 1–12 and 25–28 of the 28-line "Bridal Tribute," a poem published in *Woman's Exponent,* February 1, 1885. See *Complete Poetry,* 1013–14.
41. Snow, *Biography and Family Record,* 453–54, 461–63, 486.

Till you fulfil your great desires,
In your life-labors done;
When up to all that God requires
His people shall be one.[42]

Eliza's brother Lorenzo was seventy-two years old when he was captured while in hiding at his Brigham City home, tried, and imprisoned under the 1882 anti-polygamy law known as the Edmunds Act. When the territorial governor offered him amnesty on condition that he renounce plural marriage, he replied, "I thank you, Governor, but having adopted sacred and holy principles for which we have already sacrificed property, home and life on several occasions in their defense, we do not propose, at this late hour, to abandon them because of threatened danger."[43] During his eleven months in prison, he wrote a poem to Eliza, who was then eighty-two years old and in failing health. He praised her labors, which, he said, would shine "In record kept of works of thine, / By holy scribes, in yonder sphere, / Where thou a goddess will appear." She responded with a heartfelt tribute to his long service in the Church, which had spread "a halo on the path" of her own life.[44] The *Deseret News* published the two poems together, under the title "A Brother's and a Sister's Love, Respectfully and Expressively Painted in Poetry." Here is Eliza's tribute to her imprisoned brother:

THE RESPONSE

Hon. L. Snow:

Your precious letter, Brother Dear,
So kind, so loving, drew a tear
From eyes whence tears refuse to flow
Except for others' weal or woe.

---

42. Lines 13–20 of "Our Father's Birthday," a 20-line poem published in Snow, *Biography and Family Record,* 465–66. See *Complete Poetry,* 1004–5.

43. Romney, *Life of Lorenzo Snow,* 361.

44. Lorenzo Snow's poem was published in *Deseret News,* November 3, 1886. See *Complete Poetry,* 1267–68.

The tall expressions drawn by thee
Seem far too grand t' apply to me;
But I admit all, all is true,
As you portray'd my love for you.

Your upright course has ever spread
A halo on the path I tread:
Your firm, unwavering life, from youth
To age, has been for God and truth.

From north to south—from east to west,
Your willing feet, the sands have pressed—
O'er boist'rous seas and ocean's wave,
You've gone—for what? Men's souls to save.

In your life-record there is not
One silent page, nor one foul blot:
Eternal Archives yet will tell
Your every page is written well.

Now, in accordance with the fate
Of ancient Saints, the prison grate—
The prison walls, and prison fare
Attest your faith and patience there.

God grant us wisdom, grace and power,
To bravely stand the trying hour,
Till Zion, pure, redeem'd, and free,
Moves on in peaceful majesty.
   Lovingly, your sister,

   E. R. SNOW SMITH.[45]

---

45. Lines 1–20, 25–28, and 37–40 of "A Brother's and a Sister's Love," a 48-line poem published in *Deseret News*, November 3, 1886. See *Complete Poetry*, 1027–30.

Eliza's witness of Jesus Christ and the restoration of his gospel burned brightly. An English traveler observed in 1885: "This charming old lady, wearing her years with so grave a grace, mellowed but not humbled by time, burning with an unquenchable zeal for her strange faith, might have been proudly shown as the witness of any creed."[46] But her health was gradually failing, often vacillating. After being bedridden for weeks, she could revive and carry forth a round of visits and speeches. Then she was down again. In April 1887, eight months before her death, she received a moving letter from her longtime and dear friend Wilford Woodruff. He was in St. George (thus his reference to "my exiled lonely bed"), in hiding from federal officials who were arresting Church leaders on charges of polygamy. She was ill, and her family feared she would soon die. Woodruff frankly acknowledged her approaching death but offered words of firm assurance:

"Beloved Sister, Honored Lady, and Inspired Poetess—

"While musing upon my exiled lonely bed last night, my thoughts turned on thee, and as I cannot visit you in person, I feel disposed to use my pen. I have been informed that you are in a low state of health and perhaps not likely to recover and a prospect of your closing your labors here in the flesh, and passing on to your labors upon the other side of the Veil, I thought if that was the case, I would like to communicate with you before you left. I felt that if there is an immortal spirit dwelling in a mortal body that can lie down in death in sweet repose, it is Sister Eliza."

President Woodruff reviewed her "life and labors of love to all classes of Latter-day Saints," continuing with these words:

"I say when I reflect upon these things, I feel that you, sister Eliza, an elect Lady of the Lord, can lay down your mortal body when the time comes without a sting, a pang or a regret and pass on to your work on the other side of the Veil to a far higher state of glory where you will find a host of Patriarchs, Prophets, Apostles and Saints, as well as a large army of children who await your coming and will greet you with joy

---

46. Pfeiffer, *Flying Leaves,* 161.

and rejoicing. . . . Through the blessing of God you have been enabled to create a name and fame that will never be forgotten through all time and eternity."[47]

Eliza wrote her last poem, "Evening Thoughts," a little more than three months before her death. We might have expected a poem of personal reflection, but she chose to focus her final poetic offering on the Church and its destiny, the cause to which she had consecrated her life. Many of the lines refer to threats and calamities that faced the Church at this time. Nevertheless, as we would expect from this woman who had been an icon of faith for decades, the poem ends on a note of hope and confidence:

Evening Thoughts

The winds blow low—the winds blow high,
*   And threatening storm-clouds gather near—*
And Satan's hosts are marshal'd nigh,
*   Perchance to foul the atmosphere.*

Where, where have truth and justice fled?
*   Why are they not in session found?*
Their posts seem occupied instead,
*   By adverse spirits lurking 'round,*

But truth is true, and justice just,
*   And such they ever will remain;*
And 'tis decreed, ere long, they must
*   Return and fill their seats again.*

It seems that hell has opened wide
*   And sent its vilest imps abroad,*
To vilify, impugn, deride,
*   And persecute the Saints of God.*

---

47. Wilford Woodruff to Eliza R. Snow Smith, April 12, 1887, "Letters of Importance," in "The Heroic Pioneer," Carter, *Pioneer Heritage*, 9:281–82.

But God is God and will sustain
　　The glorious work he has begun,
Till peace shall from its rising, reign
　　Unto the setting of the sun.

An ordeal furnace near at hand,
　　Will test your faith and texture too;
But God will give you grace to stand,
　　And He will help you safely through.

And when the winds and tempests blow,
　　And the primed furnace vents its heat;
Whatever comes, 'tis yours to know,
　　Your triumph yet will be complete.

O that we all would watch and pray,
　　And ever true and faithful be—
Move on and upward day by day,
　　And nearer, O, our God, to Thee.[48]

Eliza R. Snow Smith died in the Lion House early Monday morning, December 5, 1887. *Woman's Exponent* editor Emmeline B. Wells noted that despite Sister Eliza's "failing health and waning strength"[49] in recent months, her friends could "scarcely believe she was so soon to leave them." The funeral was held in the crowd-filled Assembly Hall on Temple Square, draped in white rather than black for the occasion. She was buried in Brigham Young's private cemetery. "Eliza R. Snow Smith" is the name that appears on her gravestone, only a few yards from that of Brigham Young.

Six years before her death, Eliza had written a poem "composed for the purpose of

---

48. Lines 1–20, 25–32, and 41–44 of a 44-line poem published in *Woman's Exponent* on September 1, 1887. See *Complete Poetry,* 1040–41.

49. "Eliza Roxie Snow Smith: A Tribute of Affection," *Woman's Exponent* 16 (December 15, 1887): 108.

OPPOSITE: *Eliza's gravestone, a tribute book published after her death, and a song sheet with lyrics by E. R. Snow and music by Ebenezer Beesley.*

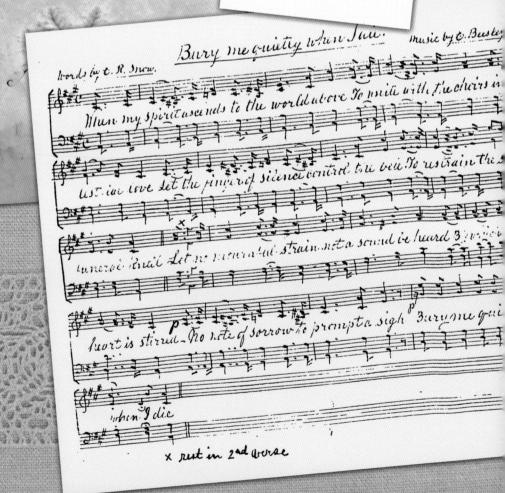

closing the history of her life,"[50] according to her friend Emmeline B. Wells. At Eliza's funeral, a choir sang these words to a tune especially composed for the occasion by Ebenezer Beesley:

Bury Me Quietly When I Die

When my spirit ascends to the world above,
To unite with the choirs in celestial love,
Let the finger of silence control the bell,
To restrain the chime of a funeral knell:
Let no mournful strain—not a sound be heard
By which a pulse of the heart is stirred—
No note of sorrow to prompt a sigh:
Bury me quietly when I die.

I am aiming to earn a celestial crown—
To merit a heavenly, pure renown;
And, whether in grave or in tomb I'm laid—
Beneath the tall oak, or the cypress shade;
Whether at home with dear friends around,
Or in distant lands, upon stranger ground—
Under wintry clouds, or a summer sky:
Bury me quietly when I die.

On the "iron rod" I have laid my hold;
If I keep the faith, and like Paul of old
Shall "have fought the good fight," and Christ the Lord
Has a crown in store with a full reward
Of the holy Priesthood in fulness rife,
With the gifts and the powers of an endless life,

---

50. "Pen Sketch of an Illustrious Woman: Eliza R. Snow Smith," *Woman's Exponent* 10 (December 1, 1881): 97.

And a glorious mansion for me on high:

Bury me quietly when I die.

Like a beacon that rises o'er ocean's wave,

There's a light—there's a life beyond the grave;

The future is bright, and it beckons me on

Where the noble and pure and the brave have gone;

Those who battled for truth with their mind and might,

With their garments clean and their armor bright:

They are dwelling with God in a world on high:

Bury me quietly when I die.[51]

Eliza's friend and first biographer, Emmeline B. Wells, attempted to assess the importance of Snow's life and poetry. "In any age or in any country she must have been a superior woman, but with the peculiar experiences of Mormonism, she is lifted far above anything she could possibly have attained in the world,"[52] wrote Wells, who was Eliza's Relief Society coworker and editor of the Latter-day Saint *Woman's Exponent.* "The gift of poesy may have been considered the highest of her intellectual qualities, but the influence for good that she exerted for the benefit of others, more especially her own sex, both by instruction and example, was what constituted her more truly great than any poem she has written."[53]

"[Eliza] was my patron saint," wrote Susa Young Gates, "and under her control and encouragement all my few literary and organizing gifts blossomed early into fruition."[54]

Orson F. Whitney expressed his feelings about Eliza's poem, "O My Father": "If all her other writings, prose and verse, were swept into oblivion, this poem alone, the

---

51. Lines 1–16, 25–32, 41–48, of a 48-line poem published in *Woman's Exponent* 10 (December 1, 1881): 97.

52. "Pen Sketch of an Illustrious Woman: Eliza R. Snow Smith," *Woman's Exponent* 9 (August 1, 1880): 33.

53. "Eliza Roxie Snow Smith: A Tribute of Affection," *Woman's Exponent* 16 (December 15, 1887): 108.

54. "Life in the Lion House," Susa Young Gates Collection, Box 12, fd. 2, p. 40, Utah State Historical Society, Salt Lake City.

sweetest and sublimest of all the songs of Zion, would perpetuate her fame and render her name immortal."[55]

Upon hearing of Eliza's death, Franklin D. Richards wrote in his journal: "Talented, pure and untiring worker for Zion."[56]

Apostle John W. Taylor paid this tribute at her funeral: "Inasmuch as the deceased was deprived of bearing children, she is entitled to be called Mother among this people, just as much as George Washington is to be called Father by the people of the United States. She has been a mother to this people. She has made us joyful by her poetical effusions; we have sorrowed when she sorrowed, and we have rejoiced when she rejoiced."[57]

Eliza R. Snow Smith, who had urged the sisters of the Church to be "holy women, full of faith and love,"[58] was just such a woman. Holiness, faith, and love marked her labors until the end of her full and remarkable life.

55. *History of Utah,* 4:573.

56. Richards, Journal, December 6, 1887, Church History Library.

57. Taylor, quoted in [Whitney,] *Life and Labors of Eliza R. Snow,* 24.

58. Line 91 of a 180-line poem published in Snow, *Biography and Family Record,* 479–83. See *Complete Poetry,* 1006–12.

SOURCES

Carter, Kate B., comp. *Our Pioneer Heritage*. 20 vols. Salt Lake City: Daughters of Utah Pioneers, 1958-77.

Davidson, Karen Lynn, David J. Whittaker, Mark Ashurst-McGee, and Richard L. Jensen, eds. *Histories, Volume 1: Joseph Smith Histories, 1832–1844*. Vol. 1 of the Histories series of *The Joseph Smith Papers*, edited by Dean C. Jessee, Ronald K. Esplin, and Richard Lyman Bushman. Salt Lake City: Church Historian's Press, 2012.

Derr, Jill Mulvay. *Mrs. Smith Goes to Washington: Eliza R. Snow's Visit to Southern Utah*. St. George, Utah: Dixie State College, 2004.

Derr, Jill Mulvay, Janath Russell Cannon, and Maureen Ursenbach Beecher. *Women of Covenant: The Story of Relief Society*. Salt Lake City: Deseret Book, 1992.

Derr, Jill Mulvay, and Karen Lynn Davidson. *Eliza R. Snow: The Complete Poetry*. Provo and Salt Lake City: Brigham Young University Press and University of Utah Press, 2009.

Faithfull, Emily. *Three Visits to America*. Edinburgh: David Douglass, 1884.

Hedges, Andrew H., Alex D. Smith, Richard Lloyd Anderson, eds. *Journals, Volume 2: December 1841–April 1843*. Vol. 2 of the Journals series of *The Joseph Smith Papers*, edited by Dean C. Jessee, Ronald K. Esplin, and Richard Lyman Bushman. Salt Lake City: Church Historian's Press, 2011.

Hymns: The Church of Jesus Christ of Latter-day Saints. Revised and enlarged. Salt Lake City: Deseret Book Company for The Church of Jesus Christ of Latter-day Saints, 1948.

Hymns of The Church of Jesus Christ of Latter-day Saints. Salt Lake City: The Church of Jesus Christ of Latter-day Saints, 1985.

Jarvis, Zora Smith. *George A. Smith Family.* Provo, Utah: privately printed, 1962.

The Life and Labors of Eliza R. Snow, with a Full Account of Her Funeral Services. [Edited by Orson F. Whitney.] Salt Lake City: Juvenile Instructor Office, 1888.

Little, James A. *Biographical Sketch of Feramorz Little.* Salt Lake City: Juvenile Instructor Office, 1890.

Ludlow, Daniel H., et al. *Encyclopedia of Mormonism.* 4 vols. New York: Macmillan, 1992.

Madsen, Carol Cornwall. *In Their Own Words: Women and the Story of Nauvoo.* Salt Lake City: Deseret Book, 1994.

Our Pioneer Heritage. Compiled by Kate B. Carter. 20 vols. Salt Lake City: Daughters of Utah Pioneers, 1958–77.

Pfeiffer, Emily. *Flying Leaves from East to West.* London, 1885.

Pyper, George D. *The Romance of an Old Playhouse.* Salt Lake City: Deseret News, 1937.

Roberts, B. H. *A Comprehensive History of the Church of Jesus Christ of Latter-day Saints, Century 1.* 6 vols. Salt Lake City: Deseret Book, 1930.

Romney, Thomas C. *The Life of Lorenzo Snow, Fifth President of the Church of Jesus Christ of Latter-day Saints.* Salt Lake City: Sugarhouse Press, 1955.

Smith, Emma. *A Collection of Sacred Hymns for the Church of the Latter Day Saints.* Kirtland, Ohio: F. G. Williams & Co., 1835.

Smith, George A., Lorenzo Snow, Paul A. Schettler, and Eliza R. Snow. *Correspondence of Palestine Tourists, Comprising a Series of Letters.* Salt Lake City: Deseret News Steam Printing Establishment, 1875.

Smith, Joseph. *History of The Church of Jesus Christ of Latter-day Saints.* Edited by B. H. Roberts. 7 vols. 2d ed. rev. Salt Lake City: The Church of Jesus Christ of Latter-day Saints, 1932–51.

Snow, Eliza R. *Biography and Family Record of Lorenzo Snow.* Salt Lake City: Deseret News, 1884.

———. *The Personal Writings of Eliza Roxcy Snow.* Edited by Maureen Ursenbach Beecher. Logan, Utah: Utah State University Press, 2000.

———. *Poems: Religious, Historical, and Political* [vol. 1]. Liverpool, 1856.

———. *Poems: Religious, Historical, and Political* [vol. 2]. Salt Lake City, 1877.

Spencer, Clarissa Young, and Mabel Harmer. *Brigham Young at Home.* Salt Lake City: Deseret Book, 1940.

Walker, James B. *Experiences of Pioneer Life in the Early Settlements and Cities of the West.* Chicago: Sumner and Co., 1881.

Whitney, Orson F. *History of Utah.* 4 vols. Salt Lake City: G. Q. Cannon and Sons, 1892–1904.

ILLUSTRATIONS

Illustrations

Illustrations

INDEX

Titles of poems appear within quotation marks. First lines of complete poems or excerpts appear without quotation marks.